WHY
GRANDMOTHERS
MATTER

Photo: Anna Gordon

About the author

Naomi Stadlen works as an existential psychotherapist in private practice, specialising in seeing mothers and parent-couples. She teaches and supervises at the New School of Psychotherapy and Counselling. She runs Mothers Talking, a weekly discussion group on Zoom. Naomi is married to Anthony Stadlen. They have three children and three grandchildren. In her spare time, Naomi enjoys Wu-style Tai Chi, quick crosswords, Jewish studies, and classical music. Further details on www.naomistadlen.com

What Mothers Do – especially when it looks like nothing (2004)
How Mothers Love – and how relationships are born (2011)
What Mothers Learn – without being taught (2020)
Why Grandmothers Matter (2023)

WHY GRANDMOTHERS MATTER

Naomi Stadlen

pinter
&
martin

Why Grandmothers Matter (Pinter & Martin Why It Matters 24)

First published by Pinter & Martin Ltd 2023

©2023 Naomi Stadlen

ISBN 978-1-78066-650-1

Also available as an ebook

Pinter & Martin Why It Matters ISSN 2056-8657

Series editor: Susan Last
Index: Helen Bilton
Cover Design: Blok Graphic, London
British Library Cataloguing-in-Publication Data

A catalogue record for this book is available from the British Library.

Set in Minion

Printed and bound in the UK by Clays

This book has been printed on paper that is sourced and harvested from sustainable forests and is FSC accredited.

Pinter & Martin Ltd
6 Effra Parade
London SW2 1PS

pinterandmartin.com

Contents

To my three wonderful grandchildren:
Tovi Wen, Anya Stadlen and Antoshka Stadlen,
and two wonderful step-granddaughters,
Lily Wen and Florri Wen

Why Grandmothers Matter is not just for grandmothers. It's for everyone. We all owe a lot to grandmothers, our own and those going back to our earliest ancestors. I hope you will find, in these pages, some good reasons why.

When I first became a grandmother, I didn't see it as a new and meaningful stage in my life. It seemed to be a sign that I was ageing, which I didn't want to consider.

Since then, I've read and listened to some of the stories that grandmothers tell about their lives. Storytelling is part of what many grandmothers do. Each one has her own special narrative voice as she reflects on her life, talks to her grandchild, or is interviewed by a researcher. But, taken together, these individual voices seem to speak with a collective sound. Grandmothers are able to look back on their years, and this can give them a valuable perspective on the present.

So in *Why Grandmothers Matter* we will listen to many examples of grandmothers' voices. Some of their thoughts might sound very ordinary, but that's the point. What we call 'ordinary' may reveal exactly that shared outlook that we are looking for.

Some of the voices I've quoted are from my Mothers Talking and Grandmothers Talking meetings. Almost all the other quoted material comes from published sources that you can check for yourself.

There is a lot to discover. Only by gathering my thoughts to write *Why Grandmothers Matter* have I understood that becoming a grandmother means more than ageing. It's an opportunity to step into a new position and to adapt a most ancient role.

1

The grandmother hypothesis

Grandmothers have a mysterious power.

It's not obvious. After all, many grandmothers today were born at times when patriarchy was the norm. The power of patriarchal fathers and grandfathers was evident to everyone. A grandfather would pass on his surname to his children and to his sons' children. He might by now be retired, but once he would have been the main breadwinner, working hard to support his family. His actions were 'visible' and in the public domain.

So do we really need to spotlight grandmothers? Obviously grandfathers are important. Why not a book about grand*parents*? There is a lot we could say about both of them. But that would mean downplaying some real differences.

A grandmother's life can seem shadowy. She may be present at her grandchildren's births, or soon after. Her children may consult her, especially if her grandchild falls ill. She may be a trusted resource, if she lives near enough, for babysitting and childcare.

Dramas involving a grandmother usually occur in private

settings, typically when only adult women are present. Sheila Kitzinger, the feminist childbirth educator, gives a perfect example of this kind of drama. She remembered how as a child she heard the beginning of an intriguing conversation about a cousin before being sent out of earshot: 'When cousin Rose became pregnant before marriage…all the women whispered in Gran's sitting room and we [children] were exiled to the staircase.'[1] It was for her an interesting memory of feeling excluded from something important.

Grandmothers usually know all kinds of family secrets. Who confided in them? How did they acquire such a collection of stories about so many family members? Storytelling, as we shall see, is a talent universally associated with grandmothers. 'Grandmothers teach us values by telling stories that are like an appliqué of anecdotes, riddles, parables – a fantastic collection,' remembered one appreciative adult grandson.[2]

A grandmother can use her knowledge to comfort and support her family. She may be able to remember, from all the family stories that she knows, an event in the past that can help to strengthen family members to face a present dilemma. But equally, she can use this same knowledge to do harm, to antagonise one branch of the family against another, or even to disfavour the whole lot of them.

Grandmothers have a special kind of power to 'frame' family stories. Outside the family, these may carry little meaning. But within it, they may be told and retold. They gather new meanings as social and political events change. Younger members add embellishments, so these stories grow and gain in fascination.

And yet, in the busy pace of public life, grandmothers don't *appear* to matter at all, or not obviously. Younger generations can be dismissive of the older ones. Knowledge has increased. Techniques have improved, even about such hallowed grandmotherly subjects as baby care. Young adults can hurry past the slower pace of a grandmother in the street, barely registering that she is there.

So do these older women *matter*? What does it mean, to 'matter'?

'Matter' is an interesting word. It derives from the Latin *mater* meaning mother. Then it gained an additional meaning. The Latin *materia* referred to 'wood,' not all of it but specifically 'the hard inner wood of the tree'. Over the centuries, this word spread through Europe. Today, the word 'matter' has become so useful that we couldn't do without it. We don't use it about wood any more. It's applied both to physical substances and to more abstract ones that have a symbolic 'solidity'. 'What's the *matter*?' we ask. So when we ask whether grandmothers matter, we are questioning whether they have a symbolic 'weight' or importance.

To whom, then, do grandmothers matter? To their grandchildren? And what about to their own children? To those who have children themselves, as well as those who don't? Do grandmothers matter to their husbands? Do they matter to themselves? And what about to all of us, our human society? Does one generation of grandmothers matter to later generations?

Yes, seems the best answer to each question. They matter to each of these, though their influence is not always obvious. Grandmothers *always* matter.

How far back is 'always'? A long way, according to anthropologists. We probably, each one of us, owe our existence to many hardworking grandmothers, unnamed and unknown to us.

As far back as we can tell, even in prehistoric times, grandmothers seem to have made a significant difference to the survival of their families. Sarah Blaffer Hrdy is an

American primatologist and anthropologist. She made a summary of recent first-hand research on how important grandmothers were in family relationships. She looked at primates and indigenous human tribes, and devoted a section of her book *Mothers and Others* to what anthropologists and primatologists have called 'the grandmother hypothesis'. This arose out of the work of anthropologists such as Kristen Hawkes. Hawkes raised some challenging questions. Why do humans survive into old age? What value do elderly persons have, especially grandmothers, once they have fulfilled their biological 'purpose' of producing children? Together with her colleagues, Hawkes discovered that grandmothers, especially, appear to have been a crucial asset to early human evolution. This is the essential claim of the grandmother hypothesis.[3]

So how could women continue to have a valuable role, once they were past childbearing age? Hrdy identified three critical areas: first, their knowledge of edible plants; second, their experience of childbirth and childcare; and third, what she called the grandmothers' 'stress-reducing component'. All of these, she argued, in prehistoric times, made a great difference to their families. And strangely, these three areas of usefulness sound familiar. Even in our technologically advanced societies, grandmothers fulfil similar roles today.

Earlier anthropologists didn't consider stone-age grandmothers very important, and Hrdy didn't let them off lightly:

Women past childbearing age were deemed irrelevant and of no theoretical interest. This prejudice surfaced occasionally in ethnographic descriptions of old women as 'physically quite revolting' or 'nuisances'. They were depicted as objects of ridicule – 'old hags' whose behaviour was obviously not worth studying.[4]

So what were these older women really contributing? Prehistoric tribes were nomadic and would hunt animals for food. A successful hunt would mean plenty of nutritious food for the tribe. But hunting isn't a reliable food source. How did a tribe survive when day after day the hunting parties returned with nothing? Hrdy wrote:

> For women who knew where to look and were willing to walk long distances, dig into hard earth, and carry their bounty back to camp, tubers provided a widely available if not particularly palatable source of calories when other foods were in short supply.[5]

Hrdy thought this information would be especially known to post-reproductive women. Older women were also good, she pointed out, at gathering edible plants, and – very important – remembering which of them had been proven poisonous. It was a detailed knowledge, as they had to know where to find the edible ones and to calculate precisely in what season an edible plant would be at its best. Margaret Ehrenberg, who wrote the groundbreaking *Women in Prehistory*, confirms how crucial prehistoric women were to their nomadic family groups. They would forage for plants which made up the bulk of the family diet:

> After a lifetime of watching plants growing, these women would have understood a great deal about the complicated business of plant biology: they would have recognised the young seedlings which had become fully grown crops when they returned to the same place later in the year. They would soon have realised that if there was less rain or less sunshine than usual the plants would not be so big and there would be less to eat, and they

13

would have realised also that the seeds needed to fall to the ground if more of that food was to grow in the same place the next year.[6]

Why would these women of 'post-reproductive age' take so much trouble to walk long distances, dig up tubers and observe the biology of plants? Part of the answer must have been for their own survival. A woman who had finished bringing up her children might be seen as an unnecessary burden to her family group. Even in modern indigenous societies which honour their grandmothers, there are times of hardship. Then, according to Marjorie M. Schweitzer, who researched American Indian groups, 'Some grandmothers are treated badly. This is particularly problematic when an old person becomes frail.'[7] A good way to safeguard her position must have been for a grandmother to make herself indispensable to her family group.

This dilemma hasn't changed, or not much. It isn't just an ancient problem faced by prehistoric or indigenous grandmothers. Modern grandmothers in the affluent West experience a similar anxiety, as we shall see. Each woman has moved from a central position as a mother to a more peripheral one as a grandmother. She may have an absorbing career. But how will she manage when she is older and frail? It may not be a conscious thought, but many grandmothers want to be useful to their families, not just for the families' good, but for their own.

City-dwelling grandmothers may not know about plants, but many have squirrelled away in their memories an impressive store of information in case it's needed. And they've learned how suddenly this need can arise. A grandmother could be having a peaceful afternoon with her grandchild. Then, just when her back is turned, he gives a yelp of pain.

That's when any tips she has for quick, homely remedies can be so useful. She has a good idea where to go for a reliable pharmacy, as well as for medical or dental emergencies. She may be able to do basic repairs around the home, but also know the telephone numbers of a friendly handyman, an electrician, and a plumber. She may start a sentence with: 'In my day, we always used to...' and finish with a simple tip. Her store of information may turn out to be exactly what her family needs.

When food is short, grandmothers may remember particular places where it's possible to find inexpensive supplies. In poorer societies, some grandmothers are doing what their ancestors did. In drought-stricken eastern Africa and Nepal, many walk miles to collect water for their families. They carry it back in large plastic cans. If they are too tired for the trip, the family has to manage without fresh water. These grandmothers must be indispensable.

The second area in which a grandmother's experience is invaluable is childbirth and childcare. Grandmothers have, by definition, given birth. From earliest times, many have comforted and supported their daughters and sometimes daughters-in-law, especially during childbirth. If a mother died in prehistoric times, it was usually a grandmother who took over the care of her children. Hrdy points out:

For society after society, grandmothers have been shown to influence the reproductive success of kin... Wherever populations were characterised by high average rates of child mortality, grandmothers – if available – made a difference to child survival.[8]

It's surprising how modern this sounds. Today, it is often the father who is encouraged to be in the hospital delivery room to witness the birth of his baby. This is a recent change. Traditionally, most births happened at home, the attendants were female, and for millennia the maternal grandmother would be one of them.

The new role of fathers is recent. Grandmothers may not be allowed in the delivery room any more, but many travel long distances to support the new family before or immediately after the birth. Besides, they have probably long been consulted by their expectant daughters for their experiences. Mothers seem to turn instinctively to older women rather than to their peers. If her mother isn't available, the new mother may seek out someone 'who is like a mother to me'.

Even though professionals and fathers have taken on her traditional role, there is still plenty for a paternal or maternal grandmother to do. Some stock up the parents' food cupboard, do the laundry, tidy the home and take the dog for a walk – all chores that make such a difference to new parents. Later on, they may care for their grandchildren, collecting them after school, feeding them and playing with them in the evenings. Their contributions may free up parents, especially single mothers, to do paid daytime and evening work. Many families depend on free childcare from grandmothers for their financial survival. Modern families may appear affluent, but the inside story is often much more precarious. As one American mother put it: 'The biggest problem right now is that the younger generation is all working, mom and dad, to survive. The grandparents have to jump in during the tough times.'[9] Nearly all the studies of grandparents agree that it is the grandmother who 'jumps in' more frequently.

Then there is the third area in which Hrdy recognised that grandmothers have always offered valuable help.

Kindly old grannies are a long-standing cultural stereotype. Yet researchers have only begun to zero in on the stress-reducing component of their benevolence.[10]

This, too, is recognisable today. Grandmothers often provide the stress-reducing support which helps to keep the family unit together. This is well summed up by psychology professor and grandmother, Kathleen Stassen Berger:

Grandmothers are designed to be pivotal family members, to oil the family machine and support every member.[11]

'To oil the family machine' is a good way of describing it. Innumerable grandmothers have discovered that the 'machine' really doesn't need a complete overhaul. But how is it that even a small drop of oil can keep it in working order?

Anyone who has been through motherhood to become a grandmother is experienced. One grandmother may have enjoyed the sweetness of life. Another may have grown bitter. But wherever she falls on the spectrum, a grandmother can see the limitations of what a human life can offer. She has usually become much more pragmatic than idealistic. She now recognises, for example, that there's no way a parent can be perfect. She knows that parents have to settle for a lot less than the high ideals to which they once aspired (or to which they *thought* they should aspire). She has also seen that even very self-critical mothers who feel overwhelmed by early motherhood go on to find aspects of it that they can do well.

A grandmother, from her perspective, can see all this clearly. It gives many of them a sense of calm. Mistakes happen. Misunderstandings happen. Furious quarrels happen. They've seen them all before. Grandmothers know that, in time, everyone will calm down, and the problems will look much smaller than they did in the heat of the moment. The parents may blame themselves and one another. Many grandmothers have learned what a waste of energy this is. They tend to stay out of disputes and not get drawn in.

That's the legendary patience of grandmothers. It's not like the patience of mothers. Mothers learn to be patient with difficulty. They usually have too much to do. The smallest delay in the sequence of tasks for the day can be distressing.

But many grandmothers are patient because they have no choice. Especially if they are older, their bodily systems are slowing down. Their hearts beat slower than when they were younger. When they get cold, they take longer to warm up. A cut finger or a bruised leg will heal, but will take a lot longer than before. A grandmother might like to run, especially if there is a train to catch to meet her family. But perhaps her eyesight is not as reliable as it used to be, and who wants to fall down the steps of a busy station? There'll be another train after the one she is going to miss.

Grandmothers can wait. They don't need everything the moment it occurs to them, as they did when they were younger. 'Cup of tea, Mum?' 'In a minute, love. When you're ready. I'll have mine when you get yours.' They can't eat the rich meals they used to without suffering pangs of indigestion.

But all this has an upside. Grandmothers have more time to think, and to wonder what all the hurry is for. Isn't it time, they realise, to appreciate whatever there is? It means that they can see more of what children see: the incredible beauty and wonder of life, not just in nature – such as the patterns of clouds in the sky – but in a drawing or a toy that her grandchild shows her.

A grandmother can listen to younger people stressing and complaining. But considering the larger scheme of things, which she can see more easily now, she asks herself: is life really as stressful as her children say? By the time a woman is a grandmother, she is bound to have experienced a share of suffering. It enables her to see human suffering in perspective.

Many of those comforting adages that we repeat were surely invented by grandmothers: 'Tomorrow is another day.' 'Least said, soonest mended.' 'Live and learn.' 'Ah, well.'

And so, whether rich or poor, educated or illiterate, with many grandchildren or just one, a grandmother may provide a sturdy and resilient kind of wisdom to support her family. Crises come and pass. She has learned to be calmer and to see how few situations require her intervention.

In these ways, the essential benefit of grandmothers has continued from generation to generation, for as far back as we have evidence. We are all descended from prehistoric families. We have no idea how much we owe to millions of capable grandmothers, from prehistoric times to today.

2

'Mum, we've got something to tell you'

Becoming a grandmother is involuntary. There are many mothers who long for grandchildren. But they can't make it happen. Grandmothers are a seemingly random selection from the much larger group of mothers.

Some women have always taken control of their life decisions: their choice of work, their partners, when to have children and then how many. They may expect to become grandmothers and perhaps have set aside some toys, and money. But... where are those grandchildren?[1]

If their children have steady partners, these women may nudge: 'Have you two thought about starting a family yet?' This kind of question can sound intrusive. The couple may have hardly considered having a family. They are enjoying their freedom as a couple, and feel that a baby would tie them down. But their mothers may be at 'a fork in the road'. One fork leads to much generous planning for grandchildren, while the other leads to compensatory plans to use resources differently in a life without them.

Besides, not every woman wants to tell her mother the moment she knows she's expecting. When she does a pregnancy test and discovers that it's positive, this can feel like private news between herself, her partner and their doctor. Especially if this is their first child, the two of them may decide not to tell anyone – at least not until the pregnancy seems safely established. It can feel strange to look at one another and imagine themselves mothering and fathering their own child.

When the new parents are ready, their own parents are usually top of the list to be told. Telling them often feels like sharing *their* news, and what the baby will mean for the two of them.

However, for a grandmother it can turn into *her* news. It may be the news she was waiting for. She can start to think about the coming baby and what her role will be. At last she can join her grandmother friends and not be the odd one out. Although for other women the announcement may not be welcome at all. It can come as a shock. 'It never occurred to me that I was already old enough to be a grandmother,' is a common reaction. 'I thought I probably would be – but later.'

Many women hear the news as a loss of freedom. The new grandmother may remember only too well how she felt as a new mother when she had to give up a degree of control over her old life to be available to her child. It's not a negotiated contract, agreed on by two parties. Nor is it like freelance work which allows a woman some scope to schedule her work times. Being a mother means being 'on call,' day and night, weekdays and weekends, especially during the early years. Her reward is not financial. It's in the wonder of starting a relationship with a new young person and exchanging a very special kind of love. However, the constant responsibility can feel exhausting. As the children grow up and take on more responsibility for their own lives, many mothers are thankful to have fewer family obligations. At last, they have more time to themselves. So hearing that they have become grandmothers can sound like a call back to family duties, and the loss of that new freedom.

Many women feel very guilty for such 'selfish' thoughts, but it might help to know that this is a typical response shared by many.

> *My daughter asked me for a lift. She got in the car and said: 'Don't drive just yet. I've got something to tell you. I'm pregnant!' I thought: NO! I wanted more time to... I don't know what I wanted to do. Have more freedom. But now I love my grandchild very, very much.*

> *My mother was horrified when I told her I was expecting. She didn't like the idea of being a grandmother. I don't think she ever really enjoyed it.*

The new grandmother may still be young with a busy social life. Becoming a grandmother can 'age' her. An extreme example comes from a woman who had had her daughter in her teens. Now her daughter was herself in her teens and doing the same thing.

> *I could break my daughter's neck for having this baby. I just got a new boyfriend. Now he will think I'm too old. It was bad enough being a mother so young – now a grandmother too!* [2]

Most grandmothers are told the news before the birth. But not all. If the expectant mother has a difficult relationship with her own mother, she may withhold the news, in which case her mother may discover it by chance. One such mother was working through her morning exercises when her adult son coolly informed her: 'You're a grandmother.' The new grandmother was startled, even more so because it was not her son's baby but her daughter's. Her daughter had told her brother, but had deliberately said nothing to the new grandmother herself.

And what about being told about second and third grandchildren? This, too, is unpredictable. A grandmother may wish for more, or feel exhausted at having so many. But she has no say in the number. It's not easy to pace her time, money or other resources, as she can't calculate how many grandchildren she will have, or when.

However, the first-time announcement is special. She has been given an additional identity. Like it or not, she has been moved up a generation. This has all kinds of implications for her.

There was going to be a new person in our family, someone who'd still be very young when I was very old. Someone who would give our family a new stake in the future.[3]

At first it might seem like the simple addition of a new baby in her family. But it also means that her child's latest partner is now definitely related to her for life. That includes the partner's family too. Some partners have already brought with them the children from a former relationship. They have become her step-grandchildren. Sara Ruddick put it in a nutshell. A grandmother, she wrote, is situated 'within a net of relationships.'[4]

When you fall in love, you accept the differences between you. The hormones do their work! But when you have

23

children, the differences between you come out very strongly. And when your children marry and have children, they may do things completely differently from you. You have to be careful, then, to hold your tongue. And that can be very hard.

Tensions can arise long before the grandchild is born. A pregnant mother is often extremely sensitive and emotional. One grandmother, perhaps trying to show that she felt connected to her son's embryonic baby, made a remark that her daughter-in-law found upsetting.

When I was pregnant, my mother-in-law was saying goodbye to us, and she said: 'Look after my grandchild!' I tried to look calm, but I was furious. I thought: What do you think I'm doing?

Was the mother's furious reaction in response to her mother-in-law's use of 'my' in 'my grandchild'? However kindly meant, it might sound possessive to a mother who hasn't seen her baby yet. It's a good example of how easily these new family relationships can become fraught.

Then there is the question of the baby's name. Is the grandmother allowed to make suggestions? Some children are called after a family relative.

When my son told me that he would like to name his baby Sam after my dad who had died fourteen weeks before his birth, it was amazing. It felt like our grandson Sam was a gift.[5]

And what would she like her grandchild to call her? Grandma? Nanna? Will the new parents allow her to decide? Though, once they can talk, many grandchildren invent their own names.

For women who have never known their own grandmothers, it can be difficult to become grandmothers themselves without any experience of being granddaughters.

> *It has left me on my own, starting from nothing, with no tradition to follow, avoid, live up to, improve on. With no idea really what a grandmother is – let alone how to be one.*[6]

The new grandmother has a lot to think over. Will the new parents want a lot of support? And does she feel able to give it? She may know a bit about giving birth: do they want her 'on call' for the birth itself? Or for soon after? Should she offer to do their shopping? Should she arrange time off work to be available?

A pregnant mother feels new sensations in her body. Nothing like this happens to a woman who is becoming a grandmother. She won't know about her change of role within her family until she is told. There isn't even a word for an 'expectant grandmother'. Her body doesn't change. Yet she may feel strangely different.

In our Western culture, a grandmother may be congratulated on the birth of her grandchild. But the assumption is that she is passive. A joyful event has happened *to* her. The congratulation doesn't suggest that she is changed by it.

However, other cultures, especially indigenous ones, acknowledge that this is a significant change for her. She is joining the ranks of a new group. From observing this group from the outside, she is suddenly welcomed as one of them.

Marjorie Schweitzer, who studied Native American grandmothers, writes:

[American] Indian women look forward to becoming grandmothers, and to the joys and responsibilities... 'Grandmother' is used in some communities to address any older woman. It is an expression of respect and honour.[7]

Margaret Behan, a Native American woman who is part of the Cheyenne Nation of Oklahoma on her mother's side, and half Cheyenne and half Arapahoe on her father's, became a grandmother in style.

Margaret became a grandmother seventeen years ago and received the Grandmother blessing, which is her tribe's ordination into grandmotherhood. She introduced herself to the Grandmother Council [of thirteen grandmothers in 2004] by singing the Turtle Song, a song taught to her by her grandmother.[8]

Once there is a special celebration to mark the change, it immediately looks desirable. A woman can look forward to it, and feel proud when at last she becomes eligible. After the celebration has taken place, she belongs to this new group and her social standing will be enhanced.

When there isn't any formal celebration, it can look more like a loss than a gain. Then grandmothers can look like a category of ageing women that no lively woman would want to join.

There is something almost laughable about finding myself a grandmother, I, who in so many ways, feel but a girl myself. It seems such a short time ago that I was buckling the blue leather sandals that I loved so much, all by myself for the first time. I remember so vividly the sensation of bare legs and shorts first thing in the morning. I remember my grandmother saying to my mother when I was about seven, 'She's got pretty legs' and how proud this made me feel. I remember so vividly being a little girl in a child's body; how come I'm a grandmother now?[9]

Becoming a grandmother gives us an additional identity. Girlhood can feel 'such a short time ago,' as this grandmother describes. And girlhood may be the first time we discover our special identity. Later we metamorphose into teenagers, and perhaps a more chaotic sense of ourselves. As we grow into adulthood and then motherhood, it can be quite a struggle to bring together and integrate so many different aspects of ourselves. So the news that we have become grandmothers can shake up our ideas of who we are, all over again. And adjusting to this extra identity may not happen overnight.

At sixty-one, I have grown into grandmothering a little more with every grandchild's birth… [with] every little hand that reaches out to touch me and every innocent face that tips up for a kiss. I never could have imagined the joy that my grandchildren bring to my life or that they do not ask me to be anything or anyone except myself.[10]

And although every day makes us older, it can be particularly poignant for a new grandmother.

There is a sadness attached to being a grandmother. Is it because you are no longer in the very centre of life? There is a casting-off of power, you are not so absolutely essential as you were when you were a mother with young children. It is a shedding of responsibility, a movement towards death.[11]

How sad is it to become a grandmother? Some grandmothers resist the 'casting-off of power.' A grandmother may see herself as generously stepping up to help with the baby, because she feels experienced and confident, and she can see that her daughter is hesitating and looks unsure of herself. But to the new mother, this may not seem generous at all. She may feel that her mother, or mother-in-law, doesn't trust her to care for her baby. She can feel sidelined and seen as incompetent. It may be difficult for the grandmother to get used to the idea that she is no longer the baby's mother herself. If she takes care of her grandchild, she is always *in loco parentis*. It takes time for many grandmothers to adjust to the difference.

> *I suddenly realised that my grandson wasn't my son. He was my daughter's. She was similar to me but she had her own independent style. I hadn't realised that a grandmother was different. I mean, I knew, but I was suddenly faced with the reality. I had to step back.*

> *I have learned to trust more, to stand back from my daughter now she is a mother, and to let her have her own space.*

And how much is becoming a grandmother 'a movement towards death'? Many grandmothers today feel – and look – quite young. A common remark they hear is: 'You can't be a *grand*mother! You don't look old enough.'

> *I had a problem with becoming a grandmother. I remember my own grandmother used to look wrinkled and old, and walked with a stick. I wasn't ready for that yet. I felt quite young.*

Previous generations of grandmothers might not have had the health that the present one can enjoy. The common Western image of a white-haired woman with infinite time on her hands, sipping tea from a china cup with a cat purring on her lap – today, this woman is more likely to be a great-grandmother. Great-grandmothers are still rare and now seem to occupy part of the role that grandmothers once had. Of course, a woman may be both a grandmother to one branch of her family, and a great-grandmother to another. Even so…

My sister, when helping children to learn to read, noticed that older copies of a book showing 'children having tea with grandma' depicted them sitting at a kitchen table laden with home-baked treats. Grandma, plump and rosy-cheeked, was wearing an apron, round glasses, and had her hair in a grey bun. In the new books, the illustration showed the children walking with a slim woman, beautifully coiffed and wearing a tailored business suit, as she guided them into a smart patisserie. That is how grannies have changed.[12]

Today's grandmothers may grumble about getting older, while at the same time recognising how lucky they are. In many cases, they have received more decades of relatively healthy life than many of their own grandmothers did. Their own mothers might have been beholden to their fathers for any money they might have. By contrast, these grandmothers are proud to have earned their own.

So many grandmothers today continue to be active. They seem to be creating a new place for themselves, between the roles of mothers and great-grandmothers. They have more time in which to raise their heads from all the urgent daily decisions and to see a wider spectrum of social problems. And they're not 'done' yet. They can still generate plenty of energy for action. Some continue in paid work; many care for their grandchildren while the parents do paid work; and some engage in social causes, local and international.

From mother into grandmother represents a significant shift. The woman is still a mother – but to her child, not to her grandchild. Her child still needs her. So surely there ought to be a Western way of celebrating a woman who has just become a grandmother. Perhaps a printed card she could send to her friends with the news: 'I've just been told I'm a grandmother!' or that they could send her: 'Congratulations! You're a grandmother.' Perhaps her grandmother friends could arrange a special party with music and dancing to show how alive they all feel. Or she could enjoy a champagne dinner with the grandfather, if he is alive and willing, to celebrate their new status.

It seems a massive waste of an opportunity if we, as a society, ignore the chance to celebrate this change. And there would be one significant advantage. Many new mothers complain that their own mothers, or mothers-in-law, try to compete with them over who knows better how to mother the baby. However, a grandmother-celebration would make it much easier for a grandmother to accept her own new position and to take pride in it. She could then see it as special, and essentially distinct, from the mother's role.

After all, when a woman becomes a grandmother, it's more than a private family event. She is at the start of an exciting new phase of her life. A grandmother has a valuable role to offer the whole of our society.

3

'One thing we can give as grandmothers is praise'

Can it really be true, the new grandmother thinks, that her baby, for whom she once felt so responsible, has grown up and is now the parent of a new baby, her grandchild? Because being a mother was *her* role. A child's middle-of-the-night cry of *'Mummy!'* was for her. Once she got used to it, that was the way it was. But now it will be a cry for her daughter or daughter-in-law.

If she has several children and one of them becomes a parent, this turns the others into aunts and uncles. It's fascinating for a new grandmother to see how the people she nurtured as playful young children suddenly mature into responsible adults who find ways to relate to her grandchild.

But what has become of her role? Does she still matter? She, once the hub of her family, can feel ousted. Being a grandmother may feel a good deal less essential.

A grandmother faces this new reality once her grandchild is born. At first, it can seem strange to hear her grandchild crying yet leave it to the mother to attend. Some grandmothers step in, feeling they know best. They seem unaware that they may calm the baby but upset the new mother.

> *The baby kept crying, and my mother took him and he stopped crying almost at once. It didn't do wonders for my confidence.*

However uncertain the mother looks at first, she only needs time to develop her own mothering style.

But then what is a grandmother supposed to do? What is her role in the family? Western grandmothers often find themselves having to invent it. It's no longer a familiar tradition that they can inherit. As one grandmother put it:

> *I have come to inhabit that curious grandparental emotion of instantly and deeply loving them [her grandchildren], while being aware that I occupy a place of secondary importance. I think of us, the grandparents, as providing a sort of back-up team, a well-meaning, cheerleading squad.[1]*

A new grandmother in Western society may not feel she has a recognised place in her family. Some new parents put on a show of cool confidence, leaving her with the impression that her experience is outdated. She may feel that they don't need her, and panic that she is now useless. She may dread to be seen as a family ornament, stuck on a shelf, to be invited for special occasions, but no longer required as a participating member of her family. Being someone who matters and makes a difference to the family, and perhaps the wider society too, seems to satisfy a deep human need. A person who matters, because she can be useful, elicits respect. This may be one reason why so many grandmothers strive to find ways of helping new families.

One grandmother wrote about her dilemma to an advice column. She said she wanted to fulfil her dream of retiring and was planning to buy a house beside the sea. However, she lived near her son, and he had just told her that they were expecting a baby. Because of his announcement, she questioned her dream of a seaside home. She wrote to the advice columnist to ask whether she should sacrifice her dream in order to live near her son and be available to his family. (The columnist encouraged her to buy the house by the sea as the family would enjoy relaxing visits to her there. But this answer may not have satisfied her.)

The urgency of wanting to be helpful is vividly expressed by another grandmother who remembered how she had felt just after the birth of her granddaughter:

> I must have driven them [her daughter and son-in-law] crazy. I was always rushing across town from my big empty house, bustling in and out, bringing things they didn't need, giving advice, staying too long… What I wanted was to be of use, but I didn't know how to conduct myself.[2]

The desperate urge to be useful to the new family is very common. There is a lack, today, of a secure role for a grandmother. This seems to be because of the decline of an older tradition. In many societies, there *was* a traditional role, especially for the maternal grandmother, which matched her desire to be useful precisely.

In many parts of the world, a special time was set aside for the grandmother to care for her daughter, often for 40 days, immediately after the birth. The new mother was largely confined to home, to breastfeeding, and learning to know her baby. Her own mother stayed with her, or visited daily, cooking and looking after her so that she could focus on her baby and relax her normal duties. If there were older children, the grandmother cared for them too. In many societies, there are special foods that are traditional for new mothers, which the grandmother would have been expected to prepare as well.

Many traditional Jewish, Christian and Muslim families still observe the 40-day custom. The idea of 40 days seems to have come from the Bible (*Leviticus*, chapter 12) which allows that length of time for the discharge of the lochia, the mother's vaginal bleeding after childbirth. So, for 40 days, the new mother was regarded as impure and expected to isolate herself. It sounds as if her female relatives decided to use her isolation as a chance to look after her. 'Yes, my mother stayed for the majority of the forty days with all of us,' one Iraqi-Jewish mother recalled.

Even when the daughter lives in the Muslim diaspora, many Muslim mothers living in Islamic states manage to continue observing the 40 days of grandmotherly care, since the new grandmothers often anticipate that they will be needed and travel to join their daughters after they have given birth. An Iraqi mother, who gave birth to her children in England, recorded:

> *Traditionally, daughters of Iraqi descent are provided with a forty-day window to recover both physically and emotionally postpartum. This recovery time brings along with it support for the new mother as well as care for the new-born, particularly from mothers, mothers-in-law and other female members of the family. The forty days of recovery are of a cultural and religious significance...*
> *In transitioning from womanhood to motherhood, I experienced a renewed fierce connection with my mother, stronger than ever, that was born along with my son. My mother would care for me in every possible way,*

practically and emotionally, holding me and steering me
through this new world, mothering me gently once again
whilst I re-grounded myself.[3]

In Catholic Spanish-speaking countries, these 40 days are
called the *Cuarentena*. The matriarchal Berber tribes of North
Africa also believe that the mother should be looked after at
home for the first 40 days after childbirth.[4]

There are many traditions in India. In some families, the
new mother's mother would come with food daily, then care
for the baby while her daughter bathed. After that, she would
massage her daughter's back with sweet-smelling oils. On
hot days, this must have been more than welcome. 'I looked
forward to my mother's visit every day,' one Indian daughter
remembered. 'The massage felt wonderful. I couldn't have
managed without it.' It can be a renewal of the connection
between mother and daughter.

In the Hopi tribe living in North America, the timing was
different according to the baby's position in the family. The
grandmother was needed for each birth.

The maternal grandmother is important from the very
beginning of the child's life. The infant is delivered in her
home, and she takes care of the mother during the period
of seclusion following the birth: forty days for a firstborn,
twenty days for subsequent births.[5]

One tremendous advantage of this tradition is that the
grandmother can fulfil her wish to be useful. It also suggests
a finite number of days when she is required to help. After
40 days, the new mother is expected to be stronger, to know
her baby better, and to be more ready to manage for herself.
The grandmother is then released from obligation but able to

choose how much to continue.

Surely there is a strong case for reviving this tradition. Perhaps it sounds impossible, as many grandmothers are young enough to be in paid employment and usually rely on their income. And a shortage of available grandmothers isn't only a Western problem. One researcher described a new mother in the small Pango Village, Vanuatu.

Christina tried to observe the ritual month of staying in her house and being cared for by her relatives, but it proved impossible. Many of her female relatives had jobs and could not be around to help with the work of caring for the new baby.[6]

But isn't this a short-sighted way to respond when a new member of our society is born?

In many countries, a mother has the option of taking maternity leave and, in some, a father can claim paternity leave. So might there be a case for creating a system for grandmother-leave? A grandmother could apply for a grandmother-package from her employer, perhaps an agreement to do some paid work in the evenings but to give traditional support to the new mother during the day? This might prevent the new mother from feeling abandoned and experiencing what we call postnatal depression. Her mother or mother-in-law could help her to adjust to her new responsibilities. It might not suit every mother (or mother-in-law) and daughter. But to date no formalised modern version of this traditional and well-tried '40-day' custom has been considered at all.

A grandmother today has no official right or obligation to help her family. In many countries, the 40 days conflict with government policies that encourage women to stay in paid work. As a result, many grandmothers are working full-time.

Unfortunately, we have a long way to go before the idea of official grandmother's leave is likely to receive government consideration.

If she can't be there, a grandmother might be able to arrange for special deliveries of ritual or healthy foods that her daughter or daughter-in-law might like. She might even pay for a postnatal doula or other helper to care for the mother. But for the new mother a shop delivery and even a postnatal doula might feel very different from having her own mother with her. The warmth of the grandmother's presence can't be ordered from any shop. Many new mothers long for the company of their own mothers.

A different difficulty can arise when the mother wasn't brought up with the '40-day' tradition, whereas her partner and therefore her partner's mother was.

> Hours after the birth, we got a call from my mother-in-law saying she was on our doorstep. We were still in the hospital. And she's come for the month, she's still with us. In her culture, it's what the new grandmother does. But she does weird things. Like she'd far rather I was bottle-feeding, so she could do it. And she sits really close by, almost touching, when I'm breastfeeding, just watching. I wish she wouldn't. And sometimes she just comes up when I'm holding the baby and takes her off me.

This grandmother sounds as if she was following a tradition of giving help without the mother needing to ask for it, to make the mother's life easier. She was doing what she believed a grandmother was supposed to do. However, her daughter-in-law clearly came from a culture in which she would be *asked* what kind of help she needed. So she responded politely to her husband's mother, whom she had never met before. But it must have felt a long month.

In many cultures, the grandmother's traditional role was to provide breastfeeding tips and encouragement to her daughter or daughter-in-law during the 40 days after childbirth. She would have breastfed her children herself and her experience and attitude would normalise it. Two researchers observed how important this could be:

> Grandmothers' infant feeding practices influence new mothers' decisions to initiate and continue breastfeeding. Grandmothers who breastfed transmit not only their practical knowledge of how to breastfeed but also their confidence that breastfeeding is the normal way to feed an infant.[7]

In this same tradition, grandmothers are also expected to know how to solve breastfeeding difficulties. Tips and herbal lore were especially important in rural cultures. In an account that may sound unusual to modern city mothers, a new grandmother told her daughter how she (the grandmother) had overcome a breastfeeding problem in Crete:

> I remember that [breastfeeding] was painful at first as I had cracked nipples. In the beginning I accidentally threw my baby on the bed out of the pain. The midwife suggested that I use a herb called Magiasilohorto. I was reluctant to use it because it was unfamiliar to me and I was concerned for its safety, but I was desperate for relief, so sent my mother to collect some by the stream of a nearby village. We didn't have it in our village, as it grows near water and in damp places. She made me a poultice to place on my nipples and a tea to drink; within a few days I was pain-free.[8]

There must be many herbal remedies for breastfeeding mothers that have been forgotten in recent centuries. We no longer live in a breastfeeding culture where a treasury of herbal knowledge would be passed verbally from grandmother to new mother.

Many new mothers appreciate practical help, especially from their own mothers, because they know how much their mothers can manage. If a grandmother lives too far away to provide regular hands-on help, her daughter can feel deeply deprived. 'Mum lives too far to visit. I get no support.' 'My mum lives abroad. I miss her.' 'My mum's the one person I can really trust with our baby. If she was here, she could babysit occasionally so my husband and I could have an evening out.'

Even if the grandmother lives locally, the 40 days of caring for the new mother would probably be unworkable. But might there be less structured ways for a grandmother to help?

New mothers often say how they long for adult company. A grandmother may be just the person to provide it.

My husband looked after the baby. I went shopping with my mum and it was lovely. We went mad and actually sat down for a cup of tea together.

One new grandmother described how she visited her daughter to offer practical help during the early weeks. Once there, she discovered that the daughter 'did almost all the baby care, but she said she was glad I was there as a witness.'[9]

This sounds a good use of the grandmother's time. A new mother may feel uncertain about what she is doing. Her baby is too young to reassure her that he feels well cared for. So a calm grandmother with time to witness and appreciate her daughter's mothering sounds ideal.

> *One thing we can give as grandmothers is praise. Our children may not be getting much from anyone else. We can affirm their parenting and say what we find good.*

Unfortunately some grandmothers can be so critical and negative that their daughters wouldn't want them as witnesses at all!

> *My mother criticises everything I do. She lives in my homeland, so we talk on the telephone. I could do with some support. But my partner and I are not married, and she thinks... [Tears]*

But perhaps even a critical grandmother like this one might feel her heart soften now that her daughter is a new mother caring for her grandchild. This might be an opportunity to heal their relationship.

And a critical grandmother might be better than one who has already died. She may never have known that she had a wonderful grandchild. Countless new mothers have wept for their loss.

> *My mother died when I was ten. Listening to new mothers casually mentioning their mothers being there... [Tears] I haven't got my mother. I miss her. I just wish she was here to tell me everything is all right.*

These new mothers seem more aware than those with living mothers of how important the grandmothers would have been for them.

A grandmother's reassurance is the result of experience. The next three examples give a glimpse into the wide range that a grandmother can draw on. Her understanding of babies may be better than it was when she was a young mother.

> *I saw both my daughters fall into the traps I did when I was first a mother, thinking, at six weeks old, that the baby is crying on purpose to annoy. But when you're a grandmother you see the amazing clear slate the baby is and that they're no more capable of being manipulative than adding two and two. I don't think I ever saw that as a mother.*[10]

She may also be reassuring over common children's illnesses. She has weathered some of these as a mother.

> *A grandmother can be calm because she knows some of it. When my grandson first had a fever, my son and daughter-in-law were terrified. But we [grandparents] knew: fevers come and work their way through, and once it's over the child is perfectly all right. We've been through plenty of fevers. We could be calm.*

In another very common situation, the mother may spend long hours doing paid work, while her children are with her own mother, at nursery, or at school. When she isn't working, the mother may wish she could be calmer with her children, but instead she is short-tempered and tense. Once again, the grandmother, under less pressure, can use her experience to stay calm. One Bangladeshi mother who was an immigrant in Britain observed the difference between the calm grandmothering of her mother and her own more fraught mothering.

> *She's more relaxed with them. They feel more comfortable asking about things and doing whatever... whereas if*

41

Samiha [her little daughter] was to ask me something
then she thinks I will say no or 'It's not the time now'
or this or that... oh she learns a lot with my mum, she's
wonderful with them, she loves them, they love her and
they are naughty, and when I'm telling them off she will
be telling me off, and she will be like, 'Stop telling them off
all the time, there's certain ways of telling them and they
will listen.' And you think oh they never do that but then
she will point out that, 'If you say it like this they would
have,' and then you think well she's right but we just tend
to do things quickly and not even think about it.[11]

Grandmothers, however, often have more time to think and
to review their actions. One frequent dilemma they report is
deciding when to intervene and when to stand back.

There's a fine line between being interfering and being
helpful. One day, I went over to my son's house so he and
his wife could go out for a run, or a meal, or something.
Their home looked a bit of a tip. The baby was asleep.
So I decided to clean up for them. That was definitely
perceived as criticism. But if I make soup and take them
some round, they appreciate that.

Some grandmothers remember how sensitive they used to be
as mothers, and agonise over the thoughtless words that they
can't take back.

I wanted to drop by my daughter-in-law. I telephoned first,
but I said something that was a huge mistake. I said: 'Don't
bother to tidy up specially, just because I'm coming.' Then I
thought: who says her home was such a mess that I thought
she'd have to tidy it because I was coming round?

Fortunately, her daughter-in-law didn't seem to have complained. Still, new mothers surely benefit from the sensitivity of the older generation. Because a grandmother can be *too* helpful. She can overdo it. Then she matters in a negative sense. The next three examples show how a grandmother can turn into a problem, rather than a resource.

A common pattern among grandmothers is to wish the parents would take on more adult responsibilities. At the same time, they take over so many parenting tasks themselves that the new parents are free to behave like adolescents. As one grandmother put it: 'My daughter likes to come over and hang out at our house with the kids [while the grandmother is looking after them]. But then she will sit and read a magazine.' Perhaps understandably, the grandmother resented her daughter taking it easy during these visits, and found it unfair. When the daughter finally left with her children, the grandmother would sigh: 'Thank God they are gone.' But she didn't insist on limiting what she could offer them. This pattern can arise easily if the grandmother doesn't set and maintain her own boundaries. The trouble is that if the grandmother keeps helping, her children will keep asking!

> *My children live quite near me so I have to be clear about what I can give and what I can't. My response is that if I can give it, I give it. But I can't always give it. I may be busy and not have time.*

Some grandmothers don't do much childcare, but they do buy presents. In moderation, this can be fun. But a grandmother can easily overdo it. As one said: 'I buy the grandkids clothes, toys, magazines, everything.' She continued doing this, even though her children begged her not to. A grandmother like this may have been short of money for most of her life, first as a child herself and then as a mother. Now she is earning and at last she can afford to shower her grandchildren with the treats that she used to long for. Perhaps it gives her a momentary pleasure to see the excitement and gratitude of her grandchildren as they unwrap the new clothes and toys. But her children had asked her not to give so much – so she has prioritised her own feelings over theirs, and become a problem for them.

A third problem can arise over fairness between grandchildren. A grandmother may have several children. She has no control over how many grandchildren she will have. She cannot know how many to expect. Many grandmothers want to be equally fair to all their children's children.

As grandmothers, it's important to accept the differences in the family. It can be very hard. In politics, we may think very differently from the families that our children marry into. But we can set a moral tone of acceptance for the whole family.

However, if siblings have experienced rivalry for their mother's approval as children, they may continue to be sensitive over the way their mother treats her grandchildren. Does she prefer one sibling's children to another? Does she compare her children's parenting styles? Sheila Kitzinger recognised this:

A grandmother may be unware that she is stimulating sibling rivalry and even exploiting it for her own ends, when she talks about her children, their partners and their children, and compares or contrasts personal appearance, behaviour, possessions, styles of parenting, or achievements. Even if she does not do this deliberately, siblings who are already competitive may take casual remarks as criticism.[12]

One researcher made the interesting discovery that siblings often didn't want more from their mothers for their own children. They just wanted their other siblings to have less![13]

'A wise grandmother,' wrote Sheila Kitzinger, as a grandmother herself, 'never compares one son's or daughter's partner with others in the family. She accepts them for who they are, and refuses to discuss anyone disparagingly.'[14]

The grandmother's comparisons and opinions about her children certainly matter to them and can be hurtful. It sounds a great pity that she can so easily provoke old sibling rivalries, whether deliberately or out of habit. These can then continue to the next generation.

A different generational issue can arise over moral differences. Religious observance is a good example. It can be hard for an observant grandmother to find that her children have rejected the old ways and identified as humanist and secular, or if they have converted to their partner's faith. The grandmother's ancestors may have passed down the same religious customs for generations. It can leave her feeling rejected and helpless. It looks as though her convictions don't matter.

There are ancient rituals to welcome a child into life outside the womb. Infant baptism is a good example. What can a devout Christian grandmother do when her children don't want to baptise her grandchildren? What will become of their souls, after they have died? And what harm can it do, the grandmother may think, to baptise them and give them the best possible chance in the afterlife? One Catholic great-grandmother expressed her desperation:

> *They don't baptise their kids. ...I told them it's not right.*
> *[Their grandmother] should tell them, why don't they*
> *baptise? I wish I could get one of [her sons], and just take*
> *them to be baptised. Maybe I'll do it myself.*[15]

This kind of conflict is hard to resolve. The great-grandmother or grandmother may demand that the new parents follow the old family traditions, or try offering rewards. But she can't compel them.

However, as one grandmother observed, the entire relationship depends on goodwill, on both sides.

> *All the research on grandparents emphasises that the*
> *middle generation can open or close the gates that*
> *allow access to grandchildren. Some gate-keepers forbid*
> *contact, some simply move far away, and some poison*
> *the grandmother-grandchildren relationship, creating a*
> *virtual wall instead of a physical one.*[16]

Many grandmothers experience access to their grandchildren as precarious in this way. Sadly, there are other examples when it's the grandparents who slam shut the gates and forbid members of the new family to contact them – often for religious or social reasons.

This can become a special problem when the parents separate or divorce. The grandmother may have suspected that the relationship was in trouble for some time. A grandmother may feel she should salvage the relationship, but her well-meaning suggestions can just add to the couple's problems. However, her more practical help might be welcome. Some couples are grateful for her support, especially if she can look after the children for them while they go for mediation or to consult a lawyer. She can also give the grandchildren a sense of continuity because, whatever else changes, they still have her stable presence.

Despite never changing a nappy, my first husband's mother was a terrific grandmother. She remained an involved and positive force in her grandsons' lives even after our divorce... She visited us, and rang regularly to talk to them, and to me about them.[17]

But grandmothers have no legal right to visit their grandchildren. So if one half of the divorcing couple decides to cut off all contact with the grandmother's branch of the family, she isn't even allowed to contact them in writing. She may have built up a warm rapport with her grandchildren, and cry to imagine them wondering whether she still loves them because she doesn't see them anymore. But she can't override their parent's wishes. She feels frozen out of the family that meant so much to her. Very likely she has done nothing wrong. It's just that a divorcing parent may feel bitter towards all their ex-partner's relatives.

It must be a great loss to her family if a willing grandmother is refused all communication.

When the parents are struggling, financially or in other ways, the grandmother's contribution may make all the difference. But, of course, she is ageing. She knows her children value what she gives. And she is giving all she can, but can see that it still isn't enough. She may be exhausted. But once she has undertaken to care for her grandchildren, it is a commitment to her adult children and very hard for her to say it is becoming too much.

It is not like working. You cannot possibly resign just because you do not like it. You cannot possibly say: 'I do not wish to take care of this grandchild any more. I give her back to you,' because what would my adult children do then?[18]

And a grandmother may step in for other reasons than to provide financial support. Her daughter may be seriously ill, or drug-addicted, alcoholic, or unable for other reasons to care for her children. If the father isn't available, one of the grandmothers may be next-of-kin. But she will probably have to go to court to get custody of her grandchild.

Lahoma [granddaughter], she's been with me since she was born, I guess. [My daughter] had problems with drugs, all these years. Lahoma, when she was left [by her mother], she had to go to McClaren Hall and then the court awarded her to me.[19]

Even worse, there have been tragic cases of parents who seem unable to cope. They torment their child, or one of their children, until one of them murders that child, or leaves the child to die of starvation or neglect. In these cases, social services often say that they had not been aware how serious the child's predicament had become. But it's interesting to hear how *often* a grandmother notices early warning signs. She may have tried to contact the police. Sadly, her voice is only heard when it's too late.

Other difficulties arise if a mother is imprisoned, especially if she is a single mother. Then it is often one of the grandmothers who steps in to rescue the children. 'They are better off with me,' she says.[20]

If a mother dies while her children are young, the grandmother may, just as she did in prehistoric times (see page 15), step in to take the mother's place as full-time carer, if she can. She is older now, so it can't be an easy commitment. As one exhausted grandmother expressed it:

> *There is nothing good in my life at the moment. If I sleep, I still think in the morning about the difficulties… My grandchild is sick and his mother is dead. I cope because I just have to… Sometimes it is hard, but there is nothing else that I can do… I go to church and I pray. But it is because I must do it that I just have to continue.*[21]

There are depths of feeling expressed here, by a grandmother who will care for her grandchild, whatever the cost to herself. It is moving to hear how strong these women are who take responsibility for their grandchildren even when they are ageing and much in need of comfort themselves.

It seems that a grandmother will come to the rescue and support her children when there is no one else available. In this kind of crisis, a grandmother knows that she matters. But does a grandmother depend on crises and worried parents to feel that she matters?

> *First grandmother: When your child is worried about your grandchild, and you are worried too, how much should you intervene and give advice?*
> *Second grandmother: My children often turn to me for advice. But they don't like me to say anything! They just like telling me about their children. What they really want is my approval.*

Approval is like a blessing that a grandmother can give her child, and her child's partner, if there is one. Even if she is unable to offer the mother those 40 days, even if she is too poor to give financial help or too exhausted or disabled to provide childcare, or lives too far away to be available, approval is a gift that she *can* give. And she can give it in person or remotely via a device from wherever she lives.

A grandmother may undervalue her approval as being 'nothing' and wish she could provide more. However, most new parents feel uplifted by their mother's approval of their parenting, even if the relationship has been tempestuous in the past.

If she chooses, a grandmother can have an important role for which her children hold her in high regard. She really doesn't need to see herself as a woman on the periphery of her family. Her views on the ways her children are parenting matter. A new parent may be quickly hurt by her negative evaluation of their work as parents, yet easily warmed by her understanding and praise.

So what evidence have we that a grandmother matters to her children? Their relief and gratitude for her kind words of approval are surely evidence enough.

4

'They grow
up quickly'

A grandchild must find it difficult to imagine how it feels to be a grandmother. But a grandmother, looking at her grandchild, usually starts to remember how it felt to be young herself. Her grandchild seems to have advantages that weren't thought of when she was young. She may envy her grandchild's youth and opportunities. And yet, looking back, many grandmothers reflect that their own childhoods were simpler, less technical, and with fewer choices, which meant that life decisions were easier.

It's hard enough for a child to understand that his or her mother was once a child. Even an early photo of the mother can be puzzling, as it's difficult to connect the young child in the picture to the familiar features of the mother. It is even harder to realise that this mother had a mother of her own. Some grandchildren need this strange-sounding relationship of themselves to their grandmothers to be explained to them many times. Ella Rodman Church, a 19th-century American writer, recognised the bewilderment of a young child:

'But were you ever young, grandmother? I mean… were you ever as little as I am now?' …She [the grandmother] replied: 'Yes, Emma, quite as little as you are.'[1]

For a grandmother, the connection makes sense. She has seen her daughter become pregnant, and her grandchild from babyhood on, either live or virtually, over many years. She may feel proud to be related. In the words of one researcher: 'Grandmothers sparkle when they talk about their grandkids.'[2] It's a lovely way of putting it, as if not only their eyes sparkle, but their entire beings.

A grandmother has by now got a clearer sense of fast-moving time than she had as a mother. 'They grow up quickly,' said one. 'They don't stay young for ever.' Another said: 'When you are a grandmother, you learn the washing-up and laundry can wait.' This seems to be the philosophy of many grandmothers. They are able to let go of their other commitments and prioritise their grandchildren. This wonderful slowness is just what their grandchildren need.

I think I can be more patient now than with my own children. Then I always had a packed agenda of things to do. Now I make time for my grandchildren, like waiting for them to do up their own shoes. I've learned not to rush in.

This chapter will be mostly about how grandmothers matter to their younger grandchildren, while the next will be mostly about teens and older ones. Grandmothers discover that, simply by setting aside unfinished chores when their young grandchildren are with them, they can generate a comfortable sense of time together.

It's important that the pleasure is mutual. 'The women I

interviewed,' wrote one researcher, 'nearly all shed happy tears as they talked about how much they love their grandchildren, love spending time with them, love caring for them, and love feeling loved in return.'[3]

They get you playing on the floor. I'm much fitter.

We do silly dancing and crayons.

They give you energy, though I feel tired after.

Some grandmothers are giving their grandchildren what they gave their children as mothers. But many are giving time and energy that they didn't feel able to give their own children. Perhaps being a grandmother gives permission to relax and enjoy. The experience can feel healing.

This has been one of the best times of my life, because she's [granddaughter] captured for me the things I lost in my two kids from not being able to stop at home with them.[4]

I did not get such a thrill out of my own two [children], but I was busy with the house and work. I seem to enjoy the grandkids more. I make excuses for the grandkids. Can't spoil them enough.[5]

With young grandchildren, the smallest rituals and treats go a long way, and eventually turn into memories recalled years later. Some grandmothers have grown up in much poorer circumstances than the more secure lives that their grandchildren enjoy. Two unrelated granddaughters, now grandmothers themselves, both remembered the simple ways their own grandmothers had kept them warm at night.

When I was quite small and feeling cold at bedtime, my grandmother would warm newspaper in front of the fire and wrap it round my bare feet. 'There's nothing like warm newspaper to warm you,' she'd say. Nowadays, with electric blankets, that sounds a bit ridiculous, but at the time it was gorgeous.[6]

My grandmother would always worry that we children would be cold at night. She used to come round and make sure we had dressing-gowns and slippers by our beds. It was nice to be cared for like that.

Another taught her granddaughter a very simple game. 'I don't remember what it's called, but …it's the one where you use the string to make shapes with your hands and with each other's hands.'[7] It sounds like the game I remember from school called 'Cat's Cradle', though there may be a variety of names for it. Only a short length of string is needed, and a single knot to tie the ends together. Then a pair or a circle of children stand round, hold out their fingers, and take turns to make shapes with the string, before carefully lifting the 'cradle,' with its complicated pattern, off the fingers of one child and onto the next. In the light of all the expensive toys for sale today, it's good to learn that, through a grandmother, a child can discover so much excitement and pleasure from a single length of string.

A fourth grandmother noticed that two of her granddaughters were given unequal amounts of attention. One was often ill, so relatives used to bring her presents when they visited. To the delight of the healthier granddaughter, her grandmother turned up one day with a small present for her too, saying: 'It's not your fault that you are not sick.' This simple gesture stood out in her granddaughter's memories of her, and she continued to feel grateful years later, even after becoming a grandmother herself.[8]

Another grandmother was asked to look after two of her grandchildren. It was a sudden request and she didn't have anything special to offer. So she took them to the local park.

I took my eight-year-old grandson and the six-month-old baby for a walk in the park. The baby slept the whole time. The eight-year-old knows I love trees and we had a wonderful time. He was interested in seed pods, like getting those 'helicopter' ones to fly. And we found some prickly-covered sweet chestnuts. We were both interested and it was a really special walk.

In these ways, grandmothers frequently noticed how little it took for their grandchildren to be completely happy. It didn't require a heavy outlay of money or effort. One grandmother was astonished to discover this.

At the end of an expensive and memorable week in Singapore, I asked my seven-year-old grandson which holiday activity he had most enjoyed there. 'Well, Grandma,' he said, 'the best part was when we were on the train at a busy time and you said that I could stand up and hold onto the silver pole.' [9]

It's easy for young chidren to feel overwhelmed by new experiences. It sounds as though the seven-year-old who was allowed to stand in the train and hold onto the silver pole felt in charge of himself and quite grownup.

Traditional grandmothers provide wonderful homemade food, and sometimes teach their grandchildren how to prepare family recipes. Years later, grandchildren recall tables laden with plentiful treats. But it isn't only about the food. Grandmothers may also provide an unhurried atmosphere and a warm interest in the excited anecdotes that their grandchildren tell them.

However, this stable pattern is changing. Grandmothers often work outside their homes. The traditional hospitality and reliable welcome aren't always possible.

I felt very guilty as my grandchildren were variously cared for in day nurseries, with child minders, and nannies. I questioned whether my career was more important than caring for my grandchildren while their parents worked. With a great struggle, I came to terms with the fact, as today's parents must, that we have choices. We live in different times.[10]

Should a woman force herself to be a 'good grandmother' and offer homemade bread and cakes when she has time? Mothers often feel guilty for not being able to provide 'everything', and it seems that grandmothers feel guilty too.

I think each grandmother can only bring what is natural to her. If she likes cooking, it's cooking. If she likes reading, it's books. No one should feel she's not a good grandmother if she's doing whatever she would naturally do. You can't do everything.

Besides, even when a grandmother sets aside chores and makes time for her grandchild, it doesn't guarantee a successful relationship. She can find it difficult to connect to her grandchild.

One of my [one-year-old] grandchildren hardly talks.
Talking is my main thing, so, without it, I hardly know
what to do. I love him but I sometimes feel de-skilled and
bored when we are together.

Usually, because a grandmother loves her grandchild, early
difficulties become much easier as the child grows older. The
grandmother can find pleasures that they can both enjoy.

And what about discipline? If both parents are in full
employment, they may opt for minimum rules when the
family is together. To a grandmother, this may look chaotic.
Should she step in if she sees her grandchildren behaving
in ways that she considers 'naughty'? If the parents seem to
ignore it, shouldn't she take charge? This was the old role
of Victorian grandmothers who believed it was their duty
to teach discipline to their grandchildren. And so Rose
Humphreys wrote in her preface to *Grandmother's Tales*,
published in 1885:

This little book is written for the dear Grandchildren of
the Authoress and their little friends; and she hopes the
lesson will teach them not to give way to temper; not to
tell untruths, will be taken to heart...[11]

The *Tales* are very readable, with stories within stories. True to
the Preface, the children were suitably punished for expressing
hot tempers and telling untruths. However, it's revealing to
notice that in one story several adults themselves told an
untruth. Presumably it was a case of 'Do as I say,' rather than
'Do as I do.'

Grandmothers today usually like to indulge their
grandchildren more than discipline them. But since their own
children have reached adulthood, the grandparents may have

spent years upgrading their home, which is now more elegant but less child-friendly. They may suddenly switch from being easy-going to being firmer. The reasons for this change may be obvious to the grandmother, but unpredictable and puzzling to her grandchild.

We have to teach our grandson who is nearly three some of the things that are different when he is staying in our home from when he is in his own home. Like that he cannot run with his little shoes on across our sofa.

And surely a grandmother, especially if she has brought up several children, must be weary of yet more 'tidying up'.

I'm not at all a tidy person. But now, even when my grandchildren are around, I need more peace and what I call tidiness.

The grandmother may have to teach her grandchild some new rules that he couldn't have known without her explanations. It can be easier for her to do this than for the child's mother. One grandmother observed:

I think what a child takes away from his mother is a very strong voice. It's almost as if she is speaking through a megaphone. It's very loud and strong. But I think a grandmother's voice has none of that. So a grandmother can say things to her grandchild that are easier to hear.

However, the grandmother doesn't have a free hand in disciplining her grandchildren. She is always *in loco parentis*. For some grandmothers, this is an uncomfortable position. One common instance is when a mother has very few rules but has made it absolutely clear that the grandmother should keep the few rules she has. A typical one is that she does not want her child to eat sugar. But the grandmother takes the grandchild out, buys a plethora of sweet treats, and then says: 'This is our secret. We mustn't tell your mum about this.'

Once a grandmother acts like this, she has put her young grandchild in a very difficult position. She is both encouraging the grandchild to disobey the mother and also to withhold the truth from her.

> *First mother: My mother keeps wanting to feed my son something with sugar. She knows I don't want him to have sugar. He's only nine months. I'm embarrassed. I don't know why she keeps saying it.*
> *Second mother: I think the desire to give a child something sweet goes very deep.*

Some mothers have described how their own mothers would strive for an exclusive intimate relationship with a grandchild which would turn the mother into an unwelcome outsider. The grandmother tries to win her grandchild's loyalty to her by buying the child expensive treats. That might be hard for the mother, especially if she can't afford the marionette theatre, or whatever gift the grandmother had come up with. These actions may show that the grandmother matters, but that she is misusing an opportunity. As a grandmother, there is no need for her to compete with the child's mother. There is room for both their roles. She has a special place in her grandchild's life that is uniquely her own.

One feature of their relationship is that both are growing older. While the grandchild is becoming more capable and energetic, the grandmother may tire more easily. She may find it harder to look after her grandchild for as long as she used to.

She may long for more free time and more privacy when she is not responsible for anyone else.

> *I love being a grandmother and seeing my [one-year-old] grandchild for a few hours. But now the family is staying with us, I realise – I feel bad saying this – but I love my freedom. I find them having them so close is quite difficult. I like a distance.*

> *I wouldn't mind going to a [retirement] home. As much as I would like to stay in my house with my grandchildren, I don't want to look after them because, when I'm with my grandchildren, and their parents, they're gonna go out and leave me with their children. I don't want the responsibility. I think I've been responsible from day one. Now I want to be free.*[12]

So parts of their relationship may have to be renegotiated with the parents. Generally, however, young grandchildren appreciate the slower grandmotherly pace. And grandmothers admire the children as miracles who ask questions that had never occurred to them, and demand that the grandmother watch while they display their talents.

'Grandchildren,' wrote the Australian author Anne Manne, 'have a kind of distance on grandparents that their parents don't.'[13] This is borne out by many children who can relate to their grandmothers more easily than their mothers relate to their own mothers.

> *My grandmother calls my [one-year-old] daughter 'He.' I don't mind that. My grandmother is always very sweet to her and is delighted to see her. But I can see that my mother can't stand it. It reminds her that my grandmother*

*has always preferred boys, and favoured her brother over
herself.*

*A grandmother can relate to a grandchild who doesn't have
a good relationship with his mother. The grandmother can
create a safe and loving space for her grandchild.*

A mother will try to look ahead ('I hope I'm not turning my
child into a spoiled brat'), but she hasn't got the years of life
experience that a grandmother has. Becoming a grandmother
can stimulate a woman into taking a new look at her family
history, behaviour patterns passed on through the generations,
and how the family fits into the society they live in. She has a
long-distance perspective that the mother won't yet have.

In particular, she can review family patterns. Often her
children's generation rebels against her own, finding an identity
in the differences. And equally often her grandchildren's
generation sees the point of some of the older values that
interest them and they revive and upgrade these values for a
changed era.

The grandmother has also watched babies develop into
young children. She has learned a great deal. Parents may
worry about a volatile child who is easily roused to tears or
anger, who 'answers back', has sudden drastic quarrels with
their friends, and so on. However, a grandmother may see
all this as the development of a lively grandchild. A 'difficult'
child of early years doesn't mean he will be 'difficult' for
the rest of his life. So, in some families, the parents may be
troubled while the grandmother remains calm.

This can work in reverse too. Parents may value a child
who is 'so easy and no trouble at all', whereas a grandmother
might notice that the child looks pale, withdrawn, and
defeated by something.

A grandmother may be helpful because she *doesn't* worry about the concerns that the parents spend hours discussing. And she *does* ask questions that the parents may hardly have thought about, such as whether a grandchild is unusually musical or talented at sport, and could benefit from more support. Many grandmothers seem to look 'over the heads' of the parents far into the future, and, from this perspective, their grandchildren's strengths stand out clearly.

> *We have more time to think, as grandmothers. We have to think for our children. We can look ahead. They are busy with the immediate.*

This puts grandmothers in a good position to nurture their grandchildren's dreams. It's interesting to read how many grandmothers have created safe spaces for their younger grandchildren to confide in them, sharing their ambitions, such as to become astronauts, film stars, or fabulously rich. Everything seems possible.

And it's revealing to discover how many grandchildren have felt encouraged by their grandmothers' ability to listen, with faith in their futures. *Here* is the special gift that a grandmother can give. Of course she knows that her grandchild may not become the fastest runner in the world. The odds make it unlikely. But she can watch his fast sprinting down her street, share his dream, and give him the sense that she loves and believes in him.

'But [my grandson]'s always busy with his friends or computer'

It is a very common pattern for grandmothers to feel increasingly irrelevant as their grandchildren become absorbed by screens. Most grandchildren have technical expertise that is beyond their grandmother's understanding. A grandmother can sit at the family kitchen table, listening, and realise that her grandchildren, and also her children, seem to know what they are talking about, whereas she may feel lonely, lost and useless in the exchange of technological knowhow.

Fascinating to see the interplay between the family when one dines out with them. I do seem invisible – but I guess one has to come to terms with that and step back.

But what the grandmother may not realise is that, even if she is just quietly sitting there, her presence has value. She is a reminder of an older style of life. She may have a steadying effect on the speakers. So she may *feel* invisible, but the conversation would be different if she wasn't there.

Sometimes even a short exchange can go further than the grandmother may realise. One grandmother, who lived far from her grandson and communicated with him virtually, complained:

I do talk sometimes with him [grandson]. But he's always busy with his friends or computer. He walks by, waves 'Hi, Grandma,' and off he goes again![1]

She may have been hoping to have a proper conversation with him, and felt snubbed when he gave her so little time. But it's possible that, from his teenage perspective, a glance at her face can be enough to give him a warm lift of mood. He can see that he matters to her. She may be more important to him than his teenage pride would allow him to show.

Long-distance communication has completely revolution-ised life for grandmothers. It used to be a slow process, with parents taking photos of the grandchildren, getting them de-veloped at the chemist, choosing the best ones for extra cop-ies, composing an update of news to go with them, packing everything in a large envelope and queueing at the Post Office to get the package weighed, stamped and sent off. Meanwhile, at her end, the grandmother would watch her street each morning for the postman to appear. Would today bring the package she longed for? There would be a certain excitement and rhythm to her expectations, and hopefully a regular mo-ment of satisfaction.

Now, communication can be instant, no matter how far away her grandchildren live. Provided she can manage a variety of devices, a grandmother can nearly always arrange to talk to them. With her own eyes, she can see how they look, and check how they are. She can also find videos of her grandchildren on social media, rewind them, and watch them again. These aren't the same as 'live' visits. But she can discover details that no one thought important enough to tell her – such as a short video clip showing one grandchild who has learned to cycle – and this can help her to feel part of present-day events in the family.

A grandmother can take a much more active role if she lives near enough. One grandmother lived with her husband, daughter and granddaughter together in the same house. A difficult situation arose when the grandmother's teenage granddaughter chose to confide a guilty secret to her grandmother, but not to her mother.

My granddaughter was in a state. She didn't want to go back to college. She'd failed an exam, and she told me but she didn't tell her mother and she asked me not to. Her mother is my daughter, and it was very difficult for me to carry this heavy secret of hers. In the end, I said if she didn't tell her mother I would. So she told her mother, and my daughter was shocked and angry. I acted as a mediator between them. Then I heard them talking and listening to one another. So I backed off.

So the mother was shocked and angry while the grandmother seemed much calmer. The granddaughter had predicted correctly how the two of them would react, and found it easier to confess to her grandmother. Being a safe listener and then a trustworthy family mediator can be two valuable roles for a grandmother.

However, this role depends on the grandmother being fair. Unfortunately, not all grandmothers are. For example, a grandmother who, as a mother, had one favourite among her children, may go on to have a favourite grandchild too. She has a special framed photograph of her preferred grandchild prominent in her sitting room, and keeps telling the others about all the good things this grandchild has done. When the grandchildren are old enough to notice, it's a quick way to arouse a sense of unfairness. And it shows, in a very negative way, how much power the grandmother has. Through her judgements, she can hurt the less favoured grandchildren deeply.

> *My grandmother was mean to me. Like a lot of grandmothers she favoured her eldest grandchild who was my sister. She was crabby and critical and put-downy and I can't remember that I ever had a conversation with her without fear that she was going to find fault with me.*[2]

Fortunately, other grandmothers discover that they can appreciate the individual characteristics of their different grandchildren. It's not necessary to measure one up against another.

> *My grandchildren have grown into beautiful young adults. While leading different lives, they are all similar threads in the tapestry of our family.*[3]

Another role for grandparents who live near enough is to broaden the outlook of their grandchildren by setting up regular educational, cultural, sports or religious visits, such as taking an older grandchild sightseeing, to museums, to sports matches, to concerts, or to religious services. The grandchild may enjoy the familiarity of regular outings without giving them much thought. Sometimes the grandchildren reach their teens before they stop to consider how these visits have affected them. That's what happened to a Jewish teenager, Esther Sha'anan. She took for granted that she went to her grandparents for the weekly Sabbath. Then, one day, it suddenly came to her that her grandmother was an important influence on her own young life.

> *A moment when I was seventeen years old and pondering what my commitment to Torah should be remains sharply engraved in my memory....I sat in synagogue, following along the English translation [of the Hebrew Torah]. For the first time, I began to understand that the actual study of Torah could have a very real and concrete impact on my life. At that moment, I had the revelation that the words printed in the book before my eyes and at my grandmother's Shabbos table, graced by all and any who needed to be there, were not two disparate aspects of Torah. At that moment, I understood I could learn something from Torah so powerful that it could create something as magnificent as my grandmother's Shabbos table. Except that she had something even greater: she knew that truth without being able to read one verse in the original Hebrew.[4]*

Attending a synagogue service is an action in the public domain. When grandfather and granddaughter returned home, the grandmother and the Sabbath table would be waiting for them. They would then enter the private domain. Sha'anan's discovery was that her grandmother's actions in the privacy of home were at least as important as the public ones.

Sha'anan was writing for a Jewish readership so she didn't explain what she had seen her grandmother do. The 'magnificent' Shabbos, or Sabbath, table would be ready on Friday nights with a white cloth, best cutlery and crockery, and dishes of fine food, all prepared by her grandmother earlier in the day. Just before sundown, her grandmother would light two candles, symbolic of the divine properties of light, cover her eyes with her hands, and utter the ancient blessing. Later, before the meal, the grandfather would say a blessing over a cup of wine, over the washing of his hands in a bowl, and over the two loaves of Sabbath bread, all of which the grandmother had set before him. Then the meal would begin as a relaxed and sacred event. Sha'anan noticed that her grandmother had prepared enough to feed not just the family but 'all and any who needed to be there.' (There are several injunctions in the Torah to feed the stranger, the widow and the orphan.)

Judaism is very much a religion of doing. Sha'anan's discovery was that her grandmother performed good actions in the privacy of home that exactly matched the written accounts in the Torah.

How far is this a characteristic pattern in other religions too? Do the grandchildren of grandparents who practise Christian, Muslim, Hindu, Buddhist, Taoist, or Confucian rituals, as well as those of other faiths, see their grandmothers carrying out the ethics of the religion in private settings while their grandfathers have more visible public roles?

There are other lessons that children learn from their grandparents. As they change from teenage to adult, the grandmother is ageing too. She may feel young and full of energy when she is on her own. But older grandchildren can tire her. Much as she loves listening to them, they talk very fast, and she may have to ask them to repeat and explain what they have just said. And for the teenagers and young adults, as one grandmother reflected, 'we are the frontline representatives of what it means to be old.'[5] A grandmother's slowness and dated assumptions may annoy her grandchildren. But still they value something else about her. They can usually feel how much she loves them.

And without realising, a grandmother has turned into a

person of historic interest. One nonagenarian grandmother overheard her adult granddaughter exclaiming in delight at her grandmother's 'vintage clothes'. But those are just the ordinary clothes that I wear, the grandmother thought.

Feeling older makes her young grandchildren feel very precious. A very ill grandmother in her eighties explained:

> My granddaughter is the light of my life; from her I get the daily pleasure of an eleven-year-old's energy and spirit. But with that is an ongoing sadness – you will not know her when she is twenty, you will not see her even begin to live her life.[6]

Despite this grandmother's sadness, she sounds as if she has a passionate curiosity. Surely, she may think, a wonderful future awaits her granddaughter. And these hopes may sustain her granddaughter long after her admiring grandmother has died.

Unfortunately there are other older grandmothers who seem more absorbed in themselves. A grandmother like this might distress her grandchild by expressing envy of their youth, or by complaining about the faculties she no longer has – neither of which the grandchild can do anything about.

A very frail grandmother can become a problem for her family. A Western solution has been the development of institutional 'care homes' where a grandmother, or her family, can pay for professional care to ease her physical disabilities. A much older tradition, more common in Asia, is the concept of filial piety. This is the idea that, because parents look after their children and perhaps later their grandchildren, they can expect their families to be grateful and, eventually, be willing to return this care when the grandparents become old and frail. If the relationship between the generations is warm and loving, the details can be negotiated well. If it isn't, it must be difficult.

However, some Asian grandmothers today, who grew up with the tradition, don't want to require this of their children and grandchildren. This may be because they see it more as a duty and find it hard to believe in the loving side. They may also dread being a burden to their families. Besides, they are often the first generation of women to have earned enough to be able to pay for their own care. So some of them proudly challenge this concept.

> It has never crossed my mind that when I care for them [her grandchildren] they have a duty to reciprocate. This is a wrong concept. Perhaps she [her daughter] may be incapable of caring for me because of some circumstances – she may be extremely busy or have health problems. Do I stop caring for the grandchild if I know my own daughter will not or cannot care for me in the future? This is wrong.[7]

And yet, traditional customs rarely disappear. Having younger generations care for their elderly parents and grandparents sounds a good solution to the problem of caring for the elderly. It means that a frail grandmother will receive personal care from a family member who knows her.

It's not always easy. Even in the West, an adult daughter may be the only resource that the elderly grandparent can rely on. One middle-aged grandmother described how she was the only person able to provide daily care for her own mother (now a great-grandmother), when the mother's carer was ill.

> My mother has dementia. My father doesn't want her to go into a care home. But now her carer is ill. I can't get anyone else. So I have to care for her, feed her, change

> *her diapers several times a day. It's not nice. I don't enjoy*
> *doing it. I try to think of her, not as my mother, but just*
> *as a fellow being, in need of my care.*

The tradition of filial piety also ensures that daughters and sons have a chance to take responsibility, and witness how the older generation ages, before reaching that stage themselves.

Ageing and dying are important parts of how we relate to one another and how each generation negotiates the care of grandparents who become ill and frail.

> *Sometimes I feel pulled in too many directions – my*
> *parents, my kids, my grandkids, two sons-in-law.*[8]

'The last gift a parent can give her or his children is an example of failing and dying well,' wrote Sara Ruddick.[9] But this 'last gift' may not be under the parent's control.

However, a momentous change in our social attitude to death has begun. Many illnesses have changed from fatal to manageable, which means that people may decline gradually, with health issues, yet die at ripe old ages. So a new interest has arisen in the quality of a person's later years. A grandchild may get used to adapting to grandparents who may be less active but still alive.

A very old grandmother may struggle to talk. Gone is her steady voice. It has become quavery. She makes an effort to say something, but the result is a bit trite. Perhaps she holds her grandchild's arm to confide in a croaky voice: 'The most important thing... is peace.' A wealth of personal experience and thought are packed into this sentence. But the grandmother no longer has the strength to tell you how she got there. It's too late. The simple platitude is all she can pass on to her grandchild.

So grandparents often provide their grandchildren with their first impressions of the human life cycle, of growing older, becoming aged and then dying. 'Is Granny actually going to *die*?' some children ask, testing out the idea for themselves.

When a grandmother dies, it might be the first time that her grandchild experiences the death of a beloved person. '*Never see her again*' can be a difficult expression even for a teenager to understand. If it's a 'slow' dying, some parents prefer to keep their children away. Others bring their children to the hospital or hospice, or wherever else the grandmother is, to see her and perhaps to say goodbye. Children are resourceful and find ways of comforting their grandmothers.

One granddaughter brought her two-year-old daughter to see her grandmother who was dying of cancer. The two-year-old went into her great-grandmother's garden, picked some colourful flowers, and wove them into the old woman's grey hair. The grandmother was absolutely enchanted. She died a day or two later.

Another granddaughter used to visit her dying grandmother and soothe her by brushing her hair. This seemed to create a profound connection between the two. Unfortunately, she was sent away on the day when her grandmother died.

I never saw her at the end and that was painful. I didn't know what to do or what to say when they came to tell me. I just thought it was the end of my world too. But that's not true, because after death people come back to you, don't they? I can visualise her easily; she's still there. I don't actually believe in the afterlife, I have no faith, but she's here for me. When I die, that's when my grandmother will die; but not before.[10]

Often, it is only after the grandmother's death that her family recognise her pivotal importance. It was in the private domain and there may be little to show for it. It's not so much what she did as the strong quality of her presence. She was *there*.

> *The atmosphere in the house changed enormously [when the grandmother died]. She was a matriarch and when she was gone who was to take her place? She was a woman of the household and she was the head of that household, and she held things together for all of us. After she died things disintegrated.*[11]

A study of 2,000 adults, aged between 18 and over 90, revealed that two-thirds of them wished they had known more about their grandparents before they died. 'A third of us don't know what our grandparents did for a living, or that they got into all sorts of mischief that would shock their families today.'[12] 'Why didn't I think to ask her?' is the regret that so many of us are left with.

It's interesting to remind ourselves that once we grandmothers were granddaughters. Many of us may not have realised how concerned our own grandmothers were about ourselves and our futures. I remember feeling a little irritated by the intensity of my grandmothers' questions about my life. I didn't realise just how important I was to both of them.

After all, provided her grandchildren keep safe and well, a grandmother can never know their completed life stories. She is left with parts of them, and has to imagine the rest. An older grandchild may need 'space' to develop. He or she may not want to answer a deluge of questions from a curious grandmother.

How far can a grandmother today imagine the future life and career of her grandchild? To take one example, a granddaughter, herself now a grandmother, recalled her own two grandmothers, both born in Australia at the end of the 19th century. She then looked forward to consider her own history, and realised just how hard it would have been for her grandmothers to imagine.

> Work both outside and inside the home was hard, and the patriarchal culture was alive and well [in her grandmothers' day]... It would have been impossible for them [her two grandmothers] to imagine the life to be led by one of their granddaughters. That this girl – me – would finish school and attend and graduate from university, be elected to the Australian parliament, become deputy leader of the Australian Labour party...[13]

But, if a grandmother lives long enough, she will be able to witness some of her grandchild's career.

While her grandchild is young, the grandmother may have had an older person's caretaking authority over her grandchild. But the child has power of a different kind. He or she is expected to live long after the grandmother has died. He or she may have the defining words on how she will be remembered. Her story may be taken out of context and evaluated by the light of future values.

Once it was she who passed on the family stories, often with anecdotes about the different family members. Now she will pass the 'baton' to her grandchild. Has she left her grandchild with loving memories of her, or with frightening, or hurtful ones? What stories will her grandchild tell? And what questions will her grandchild ask about her life that arose too late for her to explain? How will she be remembered and represented to as yet unborn members of the family?

'As a grandmother, there are two of you'

Each child has at least two grandmothers.

As a mother, you are the only one. But as a grandmother, there are two of you. Even if the other grandmother isn't alive any more, she is still a ghost, a shadow, a presence.

This is certainly true when there are stories and memories of living and dead grandmothers. A grandmother who died young may still be called 'grandmother' by her family, even if she died before knowing that she had become one. Her story is part of the larger family one.

However, children grow up in all kinds of family structures. The identities of one or both grandmothers may be confidential, if, for example, the child was born to a surrogate mother, or was an IVF baby, or was adopted. In situations like these, the grandmother may not be aware of having grandchildren. For children in step- and blended families, there may be several grandmothers. In some traditional or tribal families, most of the older women take on grandmotherly roles. So in these families, each child may have many women to call grandmother.

Where there are two grandmothers, do they matter to one another? There is the possibility of a relationship between them, but we haven't got an English word to define their connection.

> *For me, this has been one of the great discoveries of becoming a grandmother. The Jewish culture has a word for this most important relationship describing as* makantanim *the people who are the in-laws of one's adult children. The other grandmother can be a marvellous friend, confidante and ally, or a cause of anxiety, jealousy and irritation. Some grannies hardly ever meet, or are kept apart by geographical distance or by their adult children. But since I am extremely fortunate in my* makantanim, *I know this is a relationship which can lead to friendship of a very special sort.*[1]

We tend to refer to them as the maternal or paternal grandmother. And one grandmother might refer to her opposite number as a co-grandmother or the 'other' grandmother. But none of these words sound particularly warm or friendly.

> *The 'other' grandmother – no, no, she is not other. We are lucky that we all feel as part of one family. We get together frequently and we love each other.*

In many traditional societies, the maternal and paternal grandmothers have distinct roles with customs and rituals that are passed on down the generations. It's often the maternal grandmother who has a more active role, especially when her daughter is giving birth. The paternal grandmother might be asked to help if the maternal one can't. In Western hospitals, both grandmothers are usually required to sit patiently in a waiting area until after the birth.

> *The other granny was already there [after the birth] when we got there and I was immediately jealous of her. She felt I was jealous and started thrusting the baby at me which made me feel worse.*[2]

However, co-grandmothers can find ways of supporting one another.

> *We (the two grandmothers) have been exchanging texts during the pregnancy. The birth was days after the due date, and we were in cahoots. We didn't want to interfere too much, so we communicated our worries to each other.*

> *The other grandmother, mother of the beautiful, exhausted mother, understands my adoration exactly. She… could fill in details of the birth and agree with me about this boy's extraordinary beauty.*[3]

Just as a woman can't choose whether to become a grandmother, so she can't choose her co-grandmother either. Without a specific word for their connection, it's easy for the two grandmothers to assume that they don't have a significant relationship. Whereas if we had a special word, it might help them to feel more connected. Their grandchild provides the link that joins together two branches of the family.

There can be a problem when the co-grandmothers have strong but very different views on baby care. Both then try to advise the new mother, and of course, however well-meant their intentions, their suggestions conflict. This can leave the new mother feeling anxious and confused.

The two women may not know one another before the birth of their grandchild, or even speak the same language. As one put it:

> The 'other' grandmother and I haven't got a language in common. She doesn't live near me and we don't meet very often. But it's amazing how much you can express without a common language. We understand each other!

It's a great advantage when the two grandmothers, thrown together by chance, manage to create a workable relationship.

> My son's coming to stay with us, with his wife, baby and her parents. Some people are difficult to have in the kitchen. But his mother-in-law is great. She pitches in, giving exactly the right help at the right moment.

The grandmothers may have different responses to their grandchildren's behaviour. Two co-grandmothers compared notes about their grandsons, who were now teenagers. The maternal grandmother complained: 'They don't talk to me any more, the way they used to. I ask how was their day at school, and they hardly answer.' She was probably remembering the close relationship she had when their mother – her daughter – was a teenager. Whereas the paternal grandmother had herself brought up two sons, so she had a better idea of what to expect of teenage boys. She said: 'I don't feel disconnected. They don't talk much, but that only lasts a few years. They are both very kind boys. I'm awed at how technical they are. If my phone isn't working, they will sort it out for me.'

It takes time for grandmothers to see how, for their grandchildren, differences between the two grandmothers could be an advantage.

I feel quite hurt by what I see as the brusqueness of the other grandmother. We don't have a rapport. My [toddler] grandson is exploding with language. It's wonderful to hear. And with me there's a to-and-fro flow of language. And I see her looking a bit envious, wishing she could do that. But she does things I don't. I'm glad my grandson can experience such a wide palette of personalities. I talk to my grandson a lot. She hardly talks. But she took the whole family to the beach.

If the co-grandmothers find it difficult to accept their differences, their relationship can quickly turn into rivalry.

I want to be the go-to person. I sometimes get jealous if I feel he [grandson] is spending too much time with his other grandparents.[4]

In other situations, one co-grandmother may be well-off and able to offer luxuries beyond the means of the other. The financially poorer one may be sensitive to the difference and humiliated to hear details of the better-off one.

They went down to their other grandmother's house last Sunday and... when Hayley [her granddaughter] phones me up on the Monday, it's 'Nanny got this. Nanny got that.' I was cross. 'I turned round and I said, 'Who's your best nanny then?'...Then I asked Debbie [her daughter] straight out: 'What did she give you for dinner then?' Well, Debbie says she gave them a proper dinner: two

> *boiled potatoes, two roast, a spoonful of peas and a bit*
> *of meat and gravy. I said: 'Well, where's their Yorkshire?*
> *Where's their carrots?' And then it turned out she gave*
> *them nothing for their tea!... Their other nan is what I*
> *call a 'Sunday nanny.' She'll have them down every six or*
> *seven weeks – that's a Sunday nan.*[5]

This angry tone expresses the pain of a woman who comes from generations of poverty, of families who love their children but never have enough to go round. It's not quite the same as a middle-class family that has fallen on hard times. A generationally poor grandmother can feel she has completely lost out in competition with the wealthier one.

The two grandmothers may also hold different political or religious views that they might once have been willing to discuss or reconsider, but that have become entrenched with age.

> *I was the chosen family interpreter for the two*
> *grandmothers. The most immediate concern was food*
> *preparation since Grandmother Pu loved her pork dishes*
> *and Grandmother Li forbade any pork products in the*
> *house. However, Grandmother Li hoped to convince*
> *Grandmother Pu that the healthy, delicate Muslim foods –*
> *Qingzheng cuisine – would be sufficient for her during her*
> *short stay with us. Grandmother Pu, on the other hand,*
> *had very little awareness of the importance of this issue...*
> *When the aroma of pork – the 'evil smell' – penetrated the*
> *thin walls of Grandmother Pu's room and escaped into the*
> *central courtyard, Grandmother Li became outraged.*[6]

But do two grandmothers need to be divided by their differences? Some try to keep the relationship friendly, rather than make a competitor or an enemy of the co-grandmother.

I do my best to keep everything peaceful. One of the other grandmothers [of her large family] had the grandchildren every Wednesday afternoon. I'm not as organised as that. I can't imagine having all the grandchildren visit at the same time each week. But when they come for my help, I'm there. One of the grandchildren was asked which grandmother he loved best, and he chose his other one. I try to stand back and not take things personally.

The two co-grandmothers may work as a team, if they live near enough, one taking over childcare from the other, while the other does paid work. One grandmother may be much older than the other, and in less good health, so she might be unable to help as an equal. But, as one put it, they still share a 'membership of an obscure sisterhood.'[7]

Some grandmothers form much larger teams to share out childcare, and can call on one another in time of need. Competitive comparisons may sometimes arise. But the differences may be helpful. It can be instructive to compare.

Do parents treat both grandmothers equally? Do they favour one? And on what grounds – her availability, her financial assets, her good nature, or her emotional support? If one is less favoured, or thinks that she is, she may feel bitter and excluded. She may strive to be 'useful' by trying to give practical help and advice.

One of my sons says his mother-in-law keeps giving him advice, and he can't stand it. It really annoys him. I try not to get drawn in and I say: 'She's your family. She means well. You'll have to find a way to live with it.'

81

If one or both of the grandmothers have already died, it can be a painful subject and their names hardly mentioned.

My mother's mother died before I was born, and my father's mother kept herself withdrawn from us when we were children.[8]

Not all women who are called grandmothers are biological ones. Many indigenous tribes see the children as belonging to the whole tribe. The biological grandmother may not expect to have a special connection, and a woman without a biological grandchild might feel an equal responsibility towards all the children of her tribe. '[American] Indian children have many grandmothers,' explained Marjorie Schweitzer. 'In Hopi society all the women of the grandmother's generation are the child's grandparents.'[9] In traditional Maori societies, too, grandchildren (*mokopuna*) are treasures (*taonga*) who belong to the whole tribe (*iwi*).[10] This pattern used to be much more common in Western societies than it is now.

When I had my kids we lived in streets that were real communities... We all used to know each other well, and our children would play together outside. My mum would look after my kids a lot, but the neighbours would help keep an eye on them too, and we would do the same with theirs. It was like a big family.[11]

Older women, whether biological grandmothers or with enough time to be at home, would have a welcome role in these communities. It would be interesting to discover how the responsibilities between several grandmothers are worked out. Are they clear cut, or pragmatic? And do tensions arise when one grandmother is doing more (or less) than the others?

No one has really researched the relations between co-grandmothers. Many live far apart and have little connection to one another. But surely they could matter to one another, and here there is much unused potential.

A proverb said to originate from Africa runs: 'It takes a village to raise a child.' How true is this? It's frequently repeated. But the village might take a valuable responsibility away from the child's mother. Raising her child in her own way is a mother's right, even if she decides not to exercise it. If the work is shared between a whole village, the child may miss out on the chance of developing an intimate relationship with one person. This intimacy prepares the child for other more equal relationships later on, with a close friend, and when falling in love. Without the early preparation with their mother, intimacy, which is such a common human desire, can feel much more difficult.

Wouldn't it be better to say that it takes a 'village' to support the mother? Pairs or groups of grandmothers could do this. Never before have new mothers been left to 'get on with it' as much as in Western societies today. Grandmothers know what new motherhood is like, and can draw on their life experience to ensure that the mother has simple comforts that she may need.

Not many people realise how lonely a new mother can feel, and how responsible. She often longs for another adult: not to rush efficiently around her while she is feeding her baby – doing her washing-up and other household tasks – but to sit quietly beside her, to listen to her and try to understand her. 'I'm just finishing your kitchen floor,' calls her kindly neighbour, 'and then I'll bring you a cup of tea.' 'Will you pour yourself a cup and have it with me?' 'I can't, sorry, I mustn't be late for the school pick-up.'

Clock-time, the new mother discovers, is entirely different

from 'baby' time. It would be wonderful, she thinks, if the two grandmothers set up a rota of regular visits. So much better for her than sitting alone. 'You can leave the washing-up,' she calls to her mother-in-law who has just arrived. 'Can you make us both a drink and come and sit with me?' 'Yes, of course I will!'

The grandmother has time to take in that new-mother tired and lonely face. She may recognise what it means. And then she remembers!

7
The couple relationship

A grandmother and a grandfather are much more than grandparents. That's only a part of who they are. They are a couple. Some couples have stayed together. They have weathered youthful love and storms. Their relationship has been through critical moments. They have suffered external pressures, and survived. Many of these long-term relationships were founded on love from the start. Others began from convenience, but deepened into love later on.

There are many books on grandmothers, and others on both grandparents. But they mostly explore how each, or both, relate to their children and grandchildren. What about to one another? Every relationship is a growing one. Does a grandmother still matter to the grandfather?

Once the two members of the older couple were young lovers. With age, their love may be less obvious, less visibly passionate. An outsider may see few signs of it. That's because it has gone down deep. They really know one another. They have learned a good deal about themselves and one another that is painfully imperfect. So each may complain about the foibles of the other. But their basic underlying love emerges if either is distressed. Each has learned how to comfort the other. Their love is much stronger than either may think, and it continues to develop. They may appear to pull apart, but it's not that easy. There is something enduring about an older couple who continue to value one another's company, even though they are no longer young or strong.

Sometimes two people form a couple much later in life. Typically this is after one (or both) is bereaved or divorced, and has sought a new partner. One or both may be a grandparent already. They don't always have the support of their children for this new relationship. Forming a couple late in life can be difficult anyway, as both have got used to their own ways of running their daily lives. Now each has to adjust to the other. Any opposition from their children, who may resent the sudden changes to their family, must make this process harder. On the other hand, older couples are usually more experienced at relationships than they used to be. Humour comes into it. They may be quicker to laugh at themselves and make up again after a quarrel. They may be more forgiving, and less likely to give up on one another.

It gets more complicated if the couple's adult children choose new partners. To take an imaginary example, a couple may have both a widowed daughter and a divorced son. Both already had at least one child. Both daughter and son choose new partners, so now there are, potentially at least, *five* sets of grandparent-couples: 1) Daughter and son's parents. 2) The daughter's deceased husband's parents, who may have a strong relationship with their grandchildren. 3) The daughter's new partner's parents. 4) The son's divorced wife's parents who may have a strong relationship with their grandchildren. 5) The parents of the son's new partner. This then becomes a 'blended' family with many different combinations. There are biological grandparents and step-grandparents. If they draw closer, the 'steps' usually erode, and all feel like a large family – with all the inevitable warmth, tensions and disputes this implies. In these many-sided families, the grandmothers will need time to work out their own relationships too. They may form a casual grandparents' alliance, or befriend one another in couples, or very likely create a grandmothers' alliance of support for one another.

If a grandmother was widowed and hasn't remarried, she may feel strongly that she remains half of a couple. Her late husband is important to her. Widowed grandmothers describe how often they try to imagine what their husbands would have said to them about their own relationship with their grandchildren and their concerns about them.

Having grandchildren offers new opportunities which were not possible when the grandparents were parents. Typically, the new grandmother may have undertaken more care of their children than her partner. He may have been the main wage earner. But now that he has retired, he may be free for the first time in his life to be able to relax with his family. He hasn't got her wealth of experience and may keep asking: 'Did *our* kids behave like this?' His basic questions on management and her answers enable both of them to appreciate, perhaps for the first time, how hard the grandmother worked as a mother, and how much she has learned from it.

Sometimes, grandfather and grandmother may babysit together, for example, to give the parents an evening out together. But when they discuss the evening afterwards, their traditional male and female social roles may surface. The grandfather may wonder if the parents are short of money, and question whether they are spending money wisely. Whereas the grandmother is more likely to worry about the parents' wellbeing, how exhausted they look, and what practical help she could offer to make their lives easier.

Some grandparents find it hard to agree on how they want to spend their older years. A traditional male breadwinner may have spent years looking forward to his retirement. For him, this would mean relaxation, time for travel and for enjoyment. Being 'tied down' as a helpful grandfather wasn't part of his plan. Yet his partner intends to be an active grandmother. It may be possible for both to have what they want, if they are willing to discuss it.

Without the willingness to engage in discussion, differences between the couple can look insoluble. The American writer Tillie Olsen gives a painful example in her novella, 'Tell Me a Riddle'. An elderly couple has brought up a large family in America. The novella opens when all their children have grown up, left home and had families of their own. That's when the couple, now ageing grandparents, discover they have completely different ideas for their final years.

> *For forty-seven years, they had been married. How deep back the stubborn gnarled roots of the quarrel reached, no one could say – but only now, when tending to the needs of others no longer shackled them together, the roots swelled up visible, split the earth between them, and the tearing shook even to the children, long since grown.*[1]

The quarrel was whether they should live in a cooperative for the aged (his preference) or continue living independently at home (hers). We see the couple arguing while they are vacuuming a room, she moving the noisy vacuum and turning it off so she can hear herself speak, while he is 'pushing the sofa so she could get into the corner' and 'smoothing down the rug.' Even while bitterly arguing about their future, they are cooperating in their old familiar ways of cleaning their home.

Both resent the years when they struggled and suffered while they brought up their large family during the difficult years of poverty. For a week, she would not sleep with him, and this gives us a glimpse of their married life.

He slept badly, so used to her next to him. After all the years, old harmonies and dependencies deep in their bodies; she curled to him, or he coiled to her, each warmed, warming, turning as the other turned, the nights a long embrace.[2]

As with many elderly couple relationships, there is the tenderness that outsiders may not see. After that week, however bitterly they quarrelled,

Night-times her hand reached across the bed to hold his.[3]

So even when they quarrel, there is a basic understanding between them. The older they get, the less likely they are to divorce or even to threaten it. They have grown together, and have learned to rely on one another. But how can their acute differences be resolved?

Often, each wants to be heard by the other. Now their children have left home, conversations are less interrupted and can continue to completion. Once an older couple start talking, there may be a lengthy exchange of mutual recriminations which there hadn't been time to voice before now. It can sound like an avalanche of wrongdoings and injustices on both sides. They are bound to be bitter, and the past cannot be changed. But now they can take time to acknowledge one another's different perspectives, and become aware of their respective experiences which they hadn't understood before. Listening to one another can be healing and deepen their appreciation of one another.

In these long-term relationships, each owes a great deal to the other. As one grateful grandfather put it:

She does all the cooking. I don't. We'd both be corpses if it was the other way round!

Babies have physical growth spurts and perhaps elderly people have them too. Several physical changes can arise all at once, and then nothing more for a while. So the couple patiently adjust to one another's ageing. For example, her eyes may be better for reading small print while he may be stronger when it comes to carrying shopping and helping her on the stairs.

Our society tends to marginalise older people, and a grandparent couple can feel socially unimportant. So it's interesting to see the title that three psychotherapists gave to the book they edited: *How Couple Relationships Shape Our World*. They explored many kinds of intimate couple relationships, including those of elderly grandparents.

We are concerned with the importance of our most intimate relationships in shaping our worlds: whether our couplings are same or opposite sex, whether we are married or not, whether we have children or not. The evidence now is clear: the qualities of our relationships have profound implications from our earliest years, for the emotional, cognitive and physical development of our children, to our latest years – in old age.[4]

How can an elderly couple still 'shape our world'? This idea may seem unfair to anyone who is not 'coupled'. And the couple relationship is not the only way to shape our world.

A couple relationship, at its best, can 'shape our world' by revealing the strength of love, to last right through the couple's lives. The daily exchange of loving actions makes them both stronger. This long-lasting love is not sentimental. It's moral, and depends on the honesty of the couple towards one another. With love, life keeps its colour. Both members of the couple go through individual phases of lonely darkness, but then return to a renewal of their love. They look back and rekindle memories of their children, and their early life together. They feel grateful for one another and spontaneously spread a sense of thankfulness around them. Something tender and harmonious about how they look when they are walking together communicates to other people, and moves them. This is how a grandparent couple can give a strong loving 'shape' to encounter a challenging world.

They aren't perfect. Both are ageing, both may be anxious about what lies ahead. But their honesty and ease with one another gives them a safe setting in which to share their fears and then to find comfort from one another.

We think about dying: about the last time we'll do this, and the last time we'll see that. It's unbearable. But my wife's my mate. It's wonderful to have someone you can talk to about everything.

Each sees the other in a special way. To anyone younger than themselves, they look like two elderly people, with greying hair and wrinkled skin. But, if they have known one another for several decades, each can remember the other's younger self. Each can recognise the warm smile and carefree laugh, and still feel roused sexually by the other. Touch has become very important and helps to keep one another's skin warm and responsive. To one another, they have hardly changed. So an older couple may look at each other without seeing their ageing process nearly as distinctly as younger people do.

By now, the grandparents' own parents have died. They are the senior members of the family. To younger members they may look as if they are teetering on the edge, about to topple into their graves. But, to themselves, it may not feel like that. Many still have the energy for more life. There is a kind of mellow gratitude of enjoying the sunrise of a new day.

They may want to use the years left to them to develop some independent pleasures. One of them may want to have one last sexual 'fling', perhaps to defy age and feel young again. The other might decide to make new friends, to study, or take up a hobby. Both may feel that their partner is abandoning their relationship. It may be hard to appreciate that each has a very strong urge to fulfil their unlived potential. They rely on the strength of their relationship to support them as they stretch out towards something new. Communication is essential even though, as here, vestiges of the patriarchal system may show: the grandmother is facilitating her husband in the way she must have developed decades ago.

We walk and talk all the time. Our marriage is based on it. When he's writing [a new book], we go out very early along a special walk we have and we talk.

My examples are from heterosexual grandparent couples. I hesitate to write about gay grandparents because I have only talked to a few. But their experience of ageing may be similar.

There are always more issues that arise between a grandmother and her partner, right through their oldest years. Life seems to *present* them. So although a couple may appear mellow and peaceful, their relationship continues to be a living one. It isn't finished. It seems as if every difficult aspect of their lives is exposed to encourage each to be more understanding and open. This may not be visible to anyone apart from the two of them. Between themselves, their relationship keeps developing.

8

'She [grandmother]
remembered talking
to *her* grandmother'

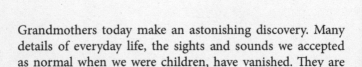

Grandmothers today make an astonishing discovery. Many details of everyday life, the sights and sounds we accepted as normal when we were children, have vanished. They are no longer part of the present. They have turned into social history.

For example, the pictorial symbol outside the men's toilet today is a figure in a pair of trousers, whereas outside the women's it's a figure in a skirt. When I was a child, this was a reflection of ordinary life. Men wore trousers while most women wore skirts. Yet this is now part of history. Most women pushing open the door of a public toilet showing the skirted figure now wear trousers. The symbol has been retained, but the reality has changed. (Today, even the concept of gendered toilets is becoming outdated.)

Some chance memories from my own childhood include the single black telephone in the hallway of many homes. It had a circular dial and loud dialling tone. An incoming call had a distinct double-ring which could be heard from every room in the home. No one shopped for milk – it was delivered, and nearly every household would have ordered milk in pint bottles for breakfast. So every morning came the slow clop-clop of the milkman's weary horse pulling the heavy jingling milk cart along the road, stopping at each building. In the evening, a brown Bakelite light switch fixed to the wall beside the door of every room was turned on with a sharp click. In the late evening, BBC radio networks closed for that day and the national anthem was played. Then it was night, with a real silence even in the city.

Today's daily life, too, will be overtaken by future developments, and become history in turn. No wonder, then, that grandmothers find it fascinating to remember details of when they were younger. Childhood is a time of constant new impressions, and a grandmother may find she can recall them vividly. Time felt different. One grandmother reflected:

> When I look back at my own childhood, like most others, I remember infinite time... The whole family [today] suffers from hurry-sickness and excess of choice and opportunity, and we are not alone.[1]

Above all, she is now the one who has inherited the family history. Hopefully she can still remember the names of family members, and some interesting anecdotes to put beside their names.

> The grandmothers are expected to pass on the critical knowledge of family connections. ...It is the grandmothers, people like me, who know exactly who is who in the complicated network of family threads.[2]

Why does family history matter? Why does any history matter? It's over, and here we are in the present. But 'the present' itself is not static. It's evolving. Our futures are uncertain, whereas the past stretches behind us, filled with complex events from which we can learn.

Yet learning from history isn't easy. Published accounts of social movements and national and international events usually summarise them in generalised and simplified language. Leading protagonists are often presented as if they knew exactly what they wanted and kept a strong control over events. The people they controlled – such as ourselves – are presented as a mass, as if we have little individual power and our precious lives are swept along by forces that are stronger than ourselves.

This is when family history can be important. It links us to individual people and the details of their past. We can see what our parents and grandparents did, and perhaps imagine how each of them felt. Their individual decisions have affected our own lives. We are continuing along a pathway of a family story that began long ago. And it's often through a grandmother that we can start to access it. Through their voices, we learn that what is history to us was reality to them. Each of us with a living grandmother can access a unique view of the past. As one grandmother put it as she looked back to her grandmother:

My grandmother's stories are important because they are the foundation of who I am. Her stories position me in a web of history and familial relations that (re)connect me to my ancestors and territory.[3]

What does it mean, to 'position me in a web of history'? A grandmother can give her grandchild a precise sense of the family's special story, of where the grandmother grew up, what influenced her, and what decisions she had to make about her life. The grandchild may learn in school history lessons about international crises, national changes, and perhaps some local events too. The grandmother's story probably weaves in and out of these, so the grandchild can see how the family story sometimes coincides with the national one but, at other times, the family opposed or was perhaps unaffected by what everyone else was doing.

Through a grandmother's memories, her grandchild can learn about moments when she had perhaps a very small but special connection to a national or international event. One English grandmother, whose parents lived in Portsmouth during the Second World War, witnessed some of the D-Day preparations just before 6 June 1944. She told her Australian grandchildren that she had been there, 'but what does this momentous event mean to them?' she asked herself. She found it hard to communicate why she had been so excited. She had seen rows of army vehicles outside her parents' house. She knew they must be significant but only later discovered that these very vehicles were to become part of the counterattack that eventually reversed the outcome of the Second World War.[4]

'I could tell them a lot about our family, but they never ask,' is a common complaint of grandmothers. Each can offer a gateway into a special family treasury of earlier family members, their struggles and their achievements.

However, if a grandchild is interested, the gates can swing open and some fascinating stories emerge. One granddaughter heard an extraordinary account of her ancient lineage from her grandmother.

When I was a teenager I talked a lot about family memories with my grandmother, my mother's mother who was in her late eighties (she was born in 1886 and died in 1975). She remembered talking to her grandmother

(who was born in 1821 and died in 1899) about her
grandmother who had been born an emigrée from the
French Revolution. My grandmother's grandmother's
grandmother remembered her grandmother who had
been a very old lady in the 1770s and had been to
Versailles either in the last years of Louis XIV or the early
years of the regency of Louis XV.[5]

It must be extraordinary to trace a family thread back like this, and perhaps to research the wider social and political contexts through which the family had lived. Each grandmother creates her life-story between her own grandparents and her grandchildren – midway in a long stretch of family history. As one grandmother saw it:

Grandparents are a doorway back into history. Their
stories of childhood and school, work and war, and of our
own parents' childhood and youth convince us that time
is real, and full of consequences.[6]

Some grandchildren are fascinated by family history, especially if there are old family photos to study. They can relate the details, such as the outdated clothes in the photos, to events they study at school. Then it becomes clear that 'time is real'. But to others it can sound too remote.

A grandmother can be an especially steady influence when the family has changed its culture, either by relocating, or by a change in social position. A Canadian granddaughter was grateful to her Jamaican grandmother.

Culture is more than food, clothes and language; it
is a way of thinking and feeling that lies at the core of
your persona... I realise that I cannot allow negative

stereotypes about Jamaicans to ruin my impression of Jamaica or make me ashamed of my background. Thankfully Yea-Yea [her grandmother] is still alive and has a great memory; she has helped me to reconcile my Jamaican heritage with my Canadian upbringing.[7]

The Australian writer and grandmother, Anne Manne, describes her mother's stories about her own mother.

We have talked a great deal about my grandmother, her domestic skills, her preserving, dressmaking, her resourcefulness, tenacity, and capacity for loving care, which held body and soul together on the impoverished farm.[8]

Through her mother's memories, Manne was able to take pride in her grandmother's resourcefulness in surviving years of hardship. Without such personal details, it can be difficult for young people today to picture such an unfamiliar way of life, when poorer women had to rely on what they could make, and were limited by the long time it took to make it. It's very different from our experience today, of purchasing food and clothes in a matter of minutes, simply by walking into a shop, or ordering grocery deliveries remotely without needing to leave home.

Again, going back two generations to another culture, one Chinese grandmother remembered her own grandmother, who was born in 1934 and later emigrated to Australia.

She mostly wore a Chinese black silk trouser suit, or a black silk Chinese dress for more formal occasions. At home, she wore black embroidered cloth shoes, encasing her tiny feet, which had been deformed from foot-binding when she was a young girl.[9]

It's possible to hear about foot-binding as an archaic custom. But the detail of this grandmother in her old age, recalling the 'black embroidered cloth shoes, encasing her tiny feet' provides a more shocking personal image that brings the custom to life.

There are family patterns that 'skip' one generation but recur in the next. Without a grandmother's recollections these might be overlooked instead of being connected to the family story.

> In a strange way, becoming a grandmother, like becoming a mother, leads you to recognise connections, characteristics and legacies of those figures from your own childhood. Your memory of the grandmother who preceded you sharpens. And the importance of them intensifies: your memory of them keeps them alive, just as their memory of their own grandparents did and still does.[10]

Many grandmothers, wherever they live, feel responsible for the memories that they carry forward into the present. They fear that all their precious details will be forgotten by the heedless ignorance of new generations. Traditional Navajo grandmothers teach their grandchildren the values of 'good thinking' and 'forward thinking'. One grandmother was trying to convey the drastic consequences she foresaw if her grandchildren did not value the teachings of traditional Navajo life.

> If the young people now, who are getting educated and so on, value the life before them, nothing will go wrong. But if they don't value it, if they are not responsible for their own thinking and their own behaviour, then there will

*not be enough to hold them together. The Navajo Nation
will then die out eventually.*[11]

The dread that grandchildren will no longer remember what
their grandmothers remember is especially poignant among
indigenous grandmothers whose children attend schools with
their expensive printed textbooks of Western history. Their
own traditions depend on the children remembering stories
communicated freely and orally to them by the previous
generation.

How does it feel to be one of the last to remember earlier
history? A Salish Indian grandmother mourned in prose that
could almost be a sorrowful song:

*Just as my mind ponders… our ancestors are no more.
Those of the Skagit River are no more. The Nooksack are
no more, where your ancestors came from. The Samish
are no more. There's not one still walking around.*[12]

The older the grandmother, the more valuable her memories.
Most grandmothers have lived through major national and
international events. This gives them a degree of perspective,
so they may be able to see social and political issues in broad
and apparently simple terms. Their children, now middle-
aged adults, may be well-informed with details. So the
grandmother's broad simplicity may appeal especially to the
understanding of her grandchildren.

However, grandmotherly experience is not childlike. It's a
distilled kind of understanding. Its apparent simplicity belies
the complex depths of experience it took the grandmother to
get there.

A generation of grandmothers

In the West, ageing is associated with loss: with physical frailty, dementia, erosion of autonomy, and more. It's rare to hear positive comments about ageing. If someone says: 'I look so *old*,' it's a complaint. It's not a source of pride.

As a generation, grandmothers will eventually become a burden to hardworking younger people. If they live long enough, they will become less active, and depend on a lot of expensive care. Typically, from having been mostly givers, they will eventually become mostly takers.

For at least a century, social planners have been warning governments to prepare for the growth of a 'top-heavy' society. 'The vision of a social system that grows top-heavy with the years and finally collapses from its own weight has haunted the minds of certain economists…' a journalist wrote in the *New York Times*. He wasn't writing recently but as long ago as 18 January 1925.

But do these older people represent only a top-heavy expense? Or can they, even at an advanced age, also be an asset? A closer look shows that they can still play an important social role. It's more obvious in times of crisis, but is equally important in our daily lives.

What happened when Covid-19 first spread and mutated worldwide? It soon became clear that older people had weaker defences against it. Some people thought at first that letting these older people die might be a natural way to solve the top-heavy problem. In theory, it might. But who, in reality, would have been happy to allow their parents and grandparents to struggle for breath and suffer horrible deaths?

With the rapid advance of Covid-19 came a shocked renewal of appreciation for grandparents. It was more than the love many people felt for their *own* ageing grandparents. There was a sudden re-evaluation of grandparents collectively, as 'the older generation'. Their immune systems were very susceptible to Covid-19. Millions died around the world during the various mutations and waves of the virus. From being a top-heavy society we suddenly risked becoming top-light. So did grandparents matter after all?

A warm affirmation came from Dr Tedros Adhanom Ghebreyesus, Director-General of the World Health Organization. In 2020, he said:

Older people carry the collective wisdom of our societies. They are valued and valuable members of our families and communities. But they are at higher risk of the more serious complications of COVID-19. We are listening to older people and those who work with and for them, to identify how best we can support them. We need to work together to protect older people from the virus, and to ensure their needs are being met – for food, fuel, prescription medication and human interaction. Physical distance doesn't mean social distance. We all need to check in regularly on older parents, neighbours, friends

*or relatives who live alone or in care homes in whatever
way is possible, so they know how much they are loved
and valued.[1]*

What kind of 'collective wisdom' did Dr Ghebreyesus mean?
Why did he say that older people are not only loved but
valued? Was he being sentimental? We talk about 'the wisdom
of old age', but is that just a cliché?

Surely not. In Britain, we discovered how real this wisdom
was in early 2020 when the first wave of Covid-19 reached
us. There was an awed recognition of its magnitude and its
capacity to destroy us all. Just as a child, faced with a new
threat, can turn to a parent for guidance, so many younger
British people turned back to history. 'The biggest crisis our
nation has faced since the Second World War...' was the
immediate comparison. So how did our forebears find their
strength and courage then?

For many, two British examples had special resonance. We
had Captain Sir Tom Moore, and we had the Queen, both
in their nineties in April 2020. Both embodied some of the
collective wisdom and calm assurance that the rest of us sought.

There was something about Captain Tom's face and bearing
that millions of people recognised instantly. He didn't seek
fame. He looked modest, disciplined, and kind. The media
quickly picked up the story of the veteran of the 'forgotten
war' in Burma. He was 99, frail, and used a walking frame.
Nevertheless, he decided to do 100 laps of his garden before
his 100th birthday at the end of April 2020, and his daughter
asked people to sponsor him. His goal was to donate the
money to the National Health Service, to express his gratitude
for the nursing he had received when he was ill. He wore his
medals as he walked, to show his pride in his country. He
was televised and his appearance moved many people deeply.

Money poured in and the total sum donated surprised all of us. It came to an astounding £33 *million*. Captain Tom, with his characteristic humility, said he was amazed at everyone for their sheer *kindness*. He thanked the nation for its generosity and said this wasn't his own doing.

So he not only demonstrated the determination and strength of an older generation, but he also expressed a warm appreciation of the younger.

The Queen too was able to inspire people through this crisis of confidence. A great-grandmother, she was still working and active. Her 'coronavirus' speech on 5 April 2020 was profoundly courageous:

> *Together we are tackling this disease, and I want to reassure you that if we remain resolute and united, then we will overcome it. I hope in the years to come everyone will be able to take pride in how they responded to this challenge. And those that come after us will say that Britons of this generation were as strong as any.*

So, like Captain Tom, she personified the strength and courage of the wartime generation. And, again like him, she was able to express her confidence in the younger generations. Both she and he recognised that those wartime qualities could be awakened in all of us to help us get through the pandemic.

It is easy to dismiss the older generation as weak and infantile – as people who need looking after because of their declining strength. Captain Tom and the Queen both reminded us of another way of seeing older people. Through their example, the reverse qualities became clear. They were looking after *us*, demonstrating that indomitable spirit that comes with having been tested, *severely* tested, without giving up. It's easy to forget that during the Second World War no one knew when, or how, it would end, as we do now. It must have seemed an endless escalation at the time. The way that whole generation responded gave us the historic example that we needed to face the pandemic, which has also seemed endless, constantly escalating, and difficult to defeat.

But when we are not in a crisis, does this generation have value? It's easy, as grandmothers, to devalue ourselves. After all, we are an increasing and international population. No longer are we a revered minority group. As we age, many of us require medical attention and daily care. Are we an expensive luxury for society to bear?

What have we, as a generation, got to offer? Even wisdom, the one positive quality associated with growing older, is no longer a source of pride. How can a grandmother compete with the internet, which can prove her ideas wrong in an instant? How wise *is* an old woman?

Sheila Kitzinger, writing about grandmothers as one herself, warns us: 'Wisdom is not an automatic gift of age... The years may bring a narrowing of vision.'[2] But could some grandmothers go the other way and *widen* their vision? Kitzinger affirmed that this was possible: 'She develops skills in diplomacy and in lateral thinking. She is wiser. In fact,' she added with spirit, 'when you become a grandmother, it is not that you grow old. It is that you grow up.'[3]

The Australian writer Helen Elliott, introducing her anthology of essays by grandmothers, had similar misgivings about the idea of the wisdom of old age:

> I don't like to use the word wisdom, because getting older doesn't mean you get any wiser, but if you are lucky, by the time you are called grandmother you find an ability to see beyond your self and perhaps have some self-perception.[4]

But does this only depend on being 'lucky'? It must be more than that. Surely, we have to work during our lifetimes for any wisdom that we can harvest. Shortly before she died, I asked my mother, a German-Jewish refugee, and by then a great-grandmother, whether old age had made her wiser. 'Wiser? No,' she said. Me: 'Surely, in ninety-six years, you must have learned so much.' She: 'Kinder. I have become kinder.' Me: 'Isn't kindness a part of wisdom?' 'No.' I asked her why not, but she was impatient at further questions. Yet surely kindness suggests a widening of perception that Kitzinger associated with wisdom.

My mother was a Jungian psychotherapist, and she was influenced by Carl Gustav Jung's understanding of wisdom. I wish I had remembered this when we had our conversation. Jung described a collective set of archetypal images that included mothers and grandmothers. Grandmother archetypes, he wrote, could attract attributes in either direction: extremes of good but also extremes of evil.

> All the fabulous and mysterious qualities attached to her [the mother's] image begin to fall away and are transferred to the person closest to her, for instance the grandmother. As the mother of the mother, she is 'greater' than the latter; she is in truth the 'grand' or 'Great Mother'. Not infrequently, she assumes the attributes of wisdom as well as those of a witch.[5]

So grandmother archetypes are associated both with wisdom and with witchlike qualities. Jung was steeped in mythology, folk tales, and anthropology. But he also had direct experience of working with elderly patients. He noticed that many of his older clients complained about the repetitive treadmill on which they found themselves. They felt stuck. He encouraged them to see that the second half of life did not have to be the same as the first. There were always opportunities for change. He saw that old age could be a wonderfully creative time.

Although Jung still has many followers, his positive view of old age – an opportunity to develop in new directions – hasn't eclipsed the widespread negative one in the West. Also, although there are plenty of older people who haven't read Jung but still use their time creatively, not even they have dispersed the cloud of gloom that hangs over ageing. The assumption is that the best of our years are over. But how can we be so sure? Is a resignation to physical decline all that our futures offer? Or are we, in the West, too negative? With so many people growing older, do we need to reset our expectations?

Because of this negative view of old age, many grandmothers focus on their losses. These tend to be physical so they are more obvious. A grandmother may overlook how much she has gained. Her gains might look like nothing, until she really thinks about them. Then she can see that she has learned a good deal, and also does have something to give back to her society.

Many grandmothers say they find it easier now than when they were mothers to relax and enjoy precious time with their grandchildren. Some are still working long shifts to make their own livings and yet squeeze in time to provide after-school childcare, enabling their adult children to work longer hours at their jobs. It sounds exhausting for these grandmothers, but many of those who say they are fully stretched find that their grandchildren give them energy and keep them feeling young. A grandmother of 67, working full-time, still found time for her four grandchildren. She said:

> *I feel extremely good, very fulfilled, and very exhausted.*
> *I feel very tired from it but go to bed with a smile on my*
> *face… Makes me feel younger… One of the worst things*

*older people can do is be by themselves with other older
people. I would rent a kid: it's the fun of it. They are so
happy when you arrive. They run to me. They call me.
We are so darn busy, it's great.*[6]

How many grandmothers 'go to bed with a smile' on their
faces after being with their grandchildren? Perhaps this is
because they can allow themselves to be slower, more patient,
and enter into carefree games.

Western society is built on the philosophy that hard work
leads to future rewards. Paradoxically, these grandmothers are
providing economic support to their societies *at the same time*
as having fun with their grandchildren. Their rewards are in
the present.

Other grandmothers focus on community roles. This is
braver than it may sound. A grandmother has seen countless
good intentions launched into action, which went on to
founder. She has heard the same aspirations voiced again and
again: '*This* time, we can't afford to fail.' And then nothing
changes. So what's the point, a grandmother may think, of
even trying?

And yet many grandmothers do try. It's interesting to read
about the range of their activities. This is not to say that every
grandmother *should* find a community project for herself. It's
not to undermine any grandmother who is feeling peaceful,
pottering about at home and enjoying television. No, by the
time a woman has become a grandmother, she has usually got
a clear idea of how she wants to live, and hopefully has the
economic means for it.

It's easy to evoke the guilty thought: 'Oh dear, I should be
doing more.' There's a book with the fine title, *Grandmother
Power,* that I found inspiring, although it also made me feel
a bit guilty for not being a socially active grandmother. Paola

Gianturco, a grandmother herself, interviewed groups of activist grandmothers from 15 countries worldwide. Each one of them wanted to make her society a better place for her grandchildren. Each was trying to put right a social injustice. Their stories are illustrated with Gianturco's full-colour photographs, which are a tremendous testament to the joy and vivacity of these high-spirited older women.

In their interviews, the grandmothers express an upsurge of energy to work for better conditions. 'I am old,' said a 65-year-old Guatemalan grandmother, 'but I feel young when I do this work.'[7] Her work was striving to protect the local children from physical and sexual abuse. 'But this work has opened up new worlds,' said an Argentinian grandmother of 61. She was a retired teacher, now concerned with introducing poorer children to the joys of reading. 'I have new friends, am reading new books, and learning new ways to teach.'[8]

One Indian grandmother was only 45. Her young age was not surprising once she explained that she had been a child bride. She married when she was just seven, and then was widowed before she was 20. She had two young sons, and had to work long hours to scrape together money that barely supported the family. She said, looking back:

> Because of my inner strength I could fight my unhappy life. We shouldn't wait for someone else to help: we should do something about it. I had sadness and many difficulties that I don't want my grandchildren to repeat. I want to give my grandchildren a good education so their lives can be smooth.[9]

Grandmother Power includes interviews with the Lolas (grandmothers) of east Asia who were forced as teenage girls to be 'comfort women' for Japanese soldiers during the Second

World War. In this role, they were repeatedly raped by the soldiers, and felt profound shame. Nevertheless, many came forward to seek justice from the Japanese government, which must have required them to recall disturbing memories of those years. In one photo, Gianturco shows a close-up photo of two Lolas, now in their eighties, able to exchange loving smiles with one another – and dancing. And, yes, even after such appalling experiences, they do look hurt but beautiful too.[10]

The significant thing about *Grandmother Power* is that none of these grandmothers was working for a government initiative or a large company. Each was part of a small grassroots group that Gianturco happened to discover. Thanks to her colourful photographs, the beauty of these grandmothers is preserved for all to see.

Another such grassroots movement is La Leche League, originally set up by seven young American mothers who were asked by other mothers how they managed to breastfeed. The seven founding mothers turned into grandmothers, and continued to work for the League. I too am a grandmother, still volunteering for the League in London. When the League celebrated its 65th anniversary, I noticed how many other British leaders were grandmothers like myself. I invited them to contribute to an article for the online journal, *65th Anniversary Magazine*. I called it 'Leaders Who Stay' and suggested they explain why they had continued to be part of the League long after their children had stopped breastfeeding. Typical grandmother comments were:

Working with new Leader Applicants provides a fruitful sense of growing the future.

Whenever I consider how I can contribute to making the world a greener place I think – help women breastfeed.

I still get such joy and satisfaction from talking to new mothers and being able to offer them support and information that may make a difference to their mothering experience, just as it did for me.[11]

Like many of the grandmothers in *Grandmother Power*, La Leche League leaders, including myself, found the warmest satisfaction in working not only for our own grandchildren, but also to keep knowledge of breastfeeding alive. It had almost died out in the United States when La Leche League started. This movement has since spread worldwide. I wish Gianturco, or someone like her, could bring her camera to meetings all over the world to make a photographic record of these remarkable La Leche League leaders.

Not all grandmothers have breastfed so, for those who haven't, La Leche League has published a tear-out sheet titled 'So Your Grandchild Is Breastfed?' There is an account of normal breastfeeding with a tactful note which might be relevant to all grandmothers, whether or not they have breastfed: 'Much of this may be different from what you learned when you had your own babies.' New mothers need lots of practical support, 'And babies still need their grandparents to love them.'[12] So all grandmothers are encouraged to recognise the value of their role.

Every active grandmother may be making a difference to a small section of her community. But collectively these differences add up. Grandmothers are a huge benefit to international society. It's hard to imagine social life without them.

Other grandmothers are thinking further ahead 'to future generations that we will never see.' These grandmothers live in indigenous tribes, connected to the land, so they are quick to observe all the changes to our planet.

These Aboriginal, Maori, American and Canadian Indian and other indigenous women were originally despised by

Western colonists, who considered them uncivilised and primitive. Now these once-despised grandmothers are gently explaining to wealthy Western civilisations how they relate to our planet. They have learned never to plunder its resources, but to make sure that whatever they take from it can be replenished. Their sensitivity and long tradition of sustainability may be the answer to Western destruction of natural resources.

I found *Grandmothers Counsel the World* on top of a wall near my home, clearly on offer to passers-by. I walked past in a hurry, and then paused. I happened to be writing a chapter on grandmothers for my book *What Mothers Learn*. Wasn't it stupid to walk past a book that seemed almost to be waiting for me? Luckily I went back and took it.

It's an account of 13 indigenous grandmothers who first met in 2004. They came from different continents and cultures, yet they shared common values and beliefs. They felt destined to come together to use the wisdom of their ancestors to guide and heal the wealthy and well-educated. For all their wealth and education, these privileged Westerners were destroying our planet, and the grandmothers believed they must be taught to respect it.

Using the simplest words, one of them, Grandmother Maria Alice, of Brazil's Amazon rainforest, said:

Although we are old ones, our voice is very important for the world at this moment. The misunderstanding in this world is that some men think they are very big. We are small ones with this love, which is the only big thing we have. We can give good words for the world. I have a very big faith that we are able to change something, that we are going to be able to give hope for our next generations.[13]

Grandmother Beatrice from Oglala Lakota in South Dakota recognised that the first change needed to be an inner one. Again, she expressed her idea in the simplest language:

> It is easy to make war. Jealousy, greed and bad feelings about people of other colours are difficult feelings to get rid of. To have peace is a great struggle. We believe that to have peace we must choose to have our thoughts be peaceful and good.[14]

Grandmother Agnes Baker Pilgrim from Grants Pass, Oregon, put her thoughts starkly:

> I am trying to teach reciprocity. We two-leggeds are always taking and rarely giving back. Without reciprocity, the balance of nature is thrown off... I am a voice for the voiceless. We are all speaking to an unseen world, speaking for our Mother Earth, trying to stop our spiritual blindness.[15]

Their voices sound strong and decisive. Each comes from an indigenous people that holds its ancestors in great respect. As a result, each woman felt like a conduit, speaking both on behalf of her revered ancestors, whom she believed could hear her, and to future generations who she hoped would benefit from her work.

So all were proud to be grandmothers. They didn't see themselves through Western eyes as old, out-of-touch and brushed aside. And their strength shows. *Grandmothers Counsel the World* contains photos of each grandmother, and several of the same women can also be seen in more recent photos in *Grandmother Power*. These grandmothers reveal a sensitive, weathered and peaceful beauty – not just in their faces but especially in their expressive hands.

A similar message is warmly communicated by an independent aboriginal grandmother, a Yorta Yorta Elder from Victoria in Australia, who is a determined cultural teacher.

> *I would like to be able to pass on whatever knowledge I have of those more than sixty thousand years of a lived culture in this country to other children as well. Aboriginal and non-Aboriginal. There is so much to know. That is why I am working with educators, and this is why I made the possum-skin cloak. If you teach children at this very intimate level, you can help to prevent racism, which seems to me to be based on nothing but ignorance.*[16]

It can be harder to convince adults. Sara Ruddick, interviewing a grandmother in the US during the Second Gulf War (2003), was thankful to hear her state: 'No grandmother would want her grandchildren to go to war. It would be unsafe.'[17]

So could grandmothers have a role, not only in wanting to protect their grandchildren from war, but also in taking actions to promote peace? War can look like a quick way for warmongers of getting something they want. But in reality few wars turn out to be quick. And they result in dreadful loss of life, destruction of buildings and countryside, followed by the growth of massive resentment on the defeated side, which often eventually leads to another war.

Indigenous societies have their own histories of conflicts. However, some have evolved more enlightened and peaceful ways of resolving these on a tribal and family level. Such smaller-scale family ways might provide a model for the larger conflicts so common in the West. After all, the Western custom of sending representatives to meet and negotiate round a table in one room means that it can feel more like a family setting, only often a 'stuck' one, with all the tensions and suspicions that arise when family members have fallen out with one another.

Some of these meetings in indigenous societies sound as if they work well. A Mexican grandmother was familiar with the process.

> *Sometimes whole families come to be cured in a ceremony; if envy or anger creates too much disturbance, the whole family will partake in a night's work. Each member of the family will reach personal understanding, will make amends, and all members will create healing rituals shared and offered during the night, until the family's harmony is restored.*[18]

One night wouldn't be enough time to resolve a larger conflict. But perhaps the wisdom gleaned from small-scale family conflicts would help in revealing how to persuade representatives of two mutually distrustful parties that they have something to gain by meeting in one room, together with an experienced team. But how can a meeting be salvaged when both sides are determined to monopolise the talking? When both sides regard listening as a sign of weakness?

There might be a role for grandmothers here who have long experience of conflicts and have learned to be patient. They may be just the ones who can ease the tension, gradually, before the talks begin. A grandmother could ask questions that would sound irrelevant and ridiculous if a negotiator asked them. 'Is your chair comfortable? I saw one as I came in that would suit a tall person like you.' 'Do you want water? Our water is very good for you.' 'Is your grandmother alive? Where does/did she live?' With light questions like these, a grandmother could persevere for a long time, until the tense atmosphere softens and there are two teams of human beings rather than two sets of robotic enemies ready to meet at the negotiating table.

One useful insight gained from conflicts on a tribal or familial scale is that there comes a point when *both* sides despair that there can be any resolution.[19] An experienced team is essential to encourage the two sides to persevere through this phase, which often seems to arise shortly before solutions become possible. Grandmothers can be both tough and very gentle. They might make an ideal team for this demanding task.

It's moving to learn about the energy that grandmothers already pour into much-needed worldwide causes. However, supposing a woman has spent her life working for her children and for her society? Suppose she is exhausted? Is social activism the only good way to live her old age?

It can't be. One woman who had thrown all her energies into caring first for her children and then for her grandchildren, ends her sad account:

> *Finally all the boys [her grandsons] were at school... I began to attend literary events again. I tried to return to the books I had started writing so long ago, but just couldn't reignite the spark. Writing needs emotional energy. Mine was extinguished... Being a grandmother had consumed me.*[20]

This account is beautifully expressed. The writing conveys emotional energy, albeit through its depletion. Perhaps her ability to write was not entirely lost.

Other grandmothers are clear about what they won't do. 'I told my children from the start that I wasn't going to be their babysitter.' 'I need my freedom. If I want to travel, that's what I'll do. I can't give up my free time for my children's families.' 'You have to insist on time for yourself. Otherwise your children will keep asking you for more.'

Many grandmothers say they crave silence and stillness, after the noise of excited grandchildren. Here is the heartfelt cry of exhaustion from another:

> *I am so tired of caring for everyone. I love them. I wanted to help them. But now I am older. I choose life. I want time to live. I just accepted it all, life rolled, but now I am done. I want a break from it all.*[21]

Surely a grandmother experiencing such profound tiredness wouldn't feel energised if she were going to meetings on climate change or teaching the local children to read. So hasn't she earned her rest? Perhaps she has enough cash to celebrate her life. In her best clothes, she could treat herself to an afternoon tea in the lounge of an old-fashioned hotel. Instead of hurrying round for her grandchildren, she could sink down into a deep armchair in the lounge area. Then she could allow a waiter to serve her while she picks up an old-style glossy magazine from the table. When she checks her phone, there are no messages. Not one. Her family really must be managing without her. Slowly she can allow her whole body to relax, knowing that she is not on call right now.

How is she benefitting our society? I would argue that she is demonstrating to all of us that a hardworking grandmother who has given so much has also earned the right to relax.

However, there are grandmothers who use their last years negatively. They feel bitter at all they have endured and communicate this to their grandchildren. A granddaughter had this to say about one of her grandmothers:

She never done anything for my mum – she was an old cow. I can see her standing there, tall, like a sergeant major; she'd frighten the life out of you as soon as look at you.[22]

There are other ways of being negative in old age. A grandmother may withdraw, feeling abandoned by her family, absorbed by her own constant critical review of how badly people have treated her. She can't stop herself thinking of all that she should and shouldn't have said to them. Her whole appearance can seem sunken and grey. Grandmothers are often good at telling stories. A lonely grandmother might easily spend her time putting together a wretched life story in which nothing ever went right for her. Maybe she chose too much safety over adventure, or too much adventure over settling down. It's easy to compare her life with others. Those other lives may look bright and brave while hers looks shrunken and poor. Fortunately in each of us is a spark and the ability to be roused from an embittered state. Life is not over. With time and perhaps an encouraging friend to help her create a more balanced life story, it is possible for such a grandmother to open out, recover self-respect, and face the world again.

What about a grandmother who is ill and in chronic pain? However good her life has been, it may already feel finished with only a slow end to life facing her. Pain can leave a woman feeling ugly and unwanted, though that may not be how she looks to others. An elderly great-grandmother, my mother, had been in a hospital bed for three months. She was receiving morphine for constant pain. On one of my visits, near the end that came as she lay in that same hospital bed, a nurse said to me: 'What I like about your mum is her smile.' 'Her smile?' 'Yes. Your mum has a lovely smile. See: *there* it is!' Sure enough, my mother's face had opened into a wide smile with shining brown eyes in a way that I hadn't seen for ages. The nurse smiled back, radiant with delight. She could see the beauty in my mother. I was very moved that my dying mother could still give so much.

'You look so young!' people say to compliment a grandmother, as if only by looking young can a woman be attractive. But a grandmother is old, or becoming so. A young person usually has a smooth skin. A grandmother's may be wrinkled and careworn from the stresses or simply from the years of her long life. Is she supposed to keep trying to look young? Can't her wrinkled and careworn face have a special kind of attraction if we learn to see it differently?

An older grandmother may lose her faculties, her sight and hearing, her ability to walk and much else. But what has she gained? Often it is a deep inner calm. She may feel this at the same time as having stressful problems to face. Even so, especially when she looks at her grandchild, she can see that her life has been fruitful. She can feel grateful for all she has been given.

So the calm expression on her face, in her gestures, in her voice – all are her legacy to her child, her grandchild and to people around her. Grandmothers can demonstrate that growing old has a positive side. In our materialist culture, which values youth, wealth, and all the social signs of success, it can be hard to notice the serenity in the face of a humble grandmother. Yet she has often gained some vital insights, less into expensive products and more into people. She has seen a lot. She has found that people are usually kind. You just have to reach them. People respond. It depends on yourself and how you talk to them.

A grandmother's face and her whole bearing can convey a vital message to her society. Old age does not have to be only a sorry process of loss. Grandmothers by their very being can remind us of all the many ways in which we gain.

Conclusion
Invisible threads

In the 'sister' book to this one, *Why Mothering Matters*, Maddie McMahon starts her introduction, not with mothers but with her own grandmother.

> *On the shelf next to me stands my grandmother's button box. It was her mother's before her, I think. The buttons inside are a historical record... Sometimes, as I take a button out to sew onto something, or throw my spare buttons in on top, I feel a visceral sense of connection through the generations; the old, work-roughened fingers, genetically related to mine, that have searched the depths of this box, seeking just the right size, shape and colour.[1]*

Why does she start with her grandmother rather than her mother? Probably because it's a good entry point to understanding a family, and then the mother's role in it. By stepping back a generation, the family dynamics become much clearer.

The tangible buttons are important too. Other grandchildren have similar tactile and visual memories, such as a grandmother's special chair; or a curiosity such as a miniature chest with tiny drawers containing dried, scented flowers from the grandmother's garden; or a set of china dolls with handmade clothes perhaps given to her when she was a child by her own grandmother. A grandchild touching her grandmother's things seems to sense something special about the history that she inherits.

I've got my grandmother's cake cutter. It's got a curved silver handle with baroque leaves, rosebuds and her initials. I never knew her. But when we have cake, I use her cake cutter and imagine her slicing a beautiful torte and serving it with coffee to her friends.

The wordless sense of touch seems important to both grandmother and grandchild. Both may enjoy stroking and hugging one another.

My grandmother was the person who could give me a hug that actually felt comforting.

Many grandchildren say they value their grandmothers for being so reliably present.

My grandmother was always there; whenever I went [to her] she was there. I can't remember going to the house when she wasn't in. She never made demands on me. I could just be with her – something stable.[2]

My grandmother was this land of safety, a presence that my sister and I could always count on. She didn't live with

us but she would come over every day and stay until my
mum got home from work. She had tremendous inner
strength and composure. Even in her seventies, her hair
was always nicely done, she wore lipstick and jewelry,
and liked fashion.

One granddaughter, already an adult, knew she could rely on
her grandmother's pride in her. She had volunteered to be on
a gameshow. She would normally have felt terrified to watch
it, but: 'When my show was on TV,' she said, 'I was sitting
in my gran's house. I knew she'd be proud of me, whatever
I'd done.' And, sitting beside her proud grandmother, she felt
pleased, rather than self-critical, at how she came across.[3]

It sounds as if both safety and warm support are qualities
that many grandchildren associate with their grandmothers.

A granddaughter might not want to reveal just how
important her grandmother is. Especially when there is a
conflict between herself and her parents, the granddaughter
may feel torn, confused, or remote. And yet younger people
often harbour a deep longing to receive what, in more religious
times, would be called a blessing from the older. The writer
Anne Manne described this need.

Despite our differences, Nan was a deeply important
presence in my life… Before my marriage, I visited her.
She was by then very old and frail, and about to leave
the home where she had spent almost all of her adult life
to live with my aunt in Queensland. Strangely enough,
despite our radical difference of temper, outlook, values
and everything else, I found myself actually wanting her
approval or blessing in some way. I wanted to persuade
her that my marriage was to the right man.[4]

Anne's grandmother wasn't easy to persuade, and made her granddaughter work hard for her approval. But Anne got the 'blessing' that she wanted for her marriage in the end.

What is this strange gift that a grandmother can bestow and that seems to matter so much to her grandchild?

George MacDonald, a 19th-century priest and writer, seemed to understand. He created a symbol of the grandmother relationship through one of his fairy tales written, he tells us, 'not for children but for the child-like, whether they be of five, or fifty or seventy-five years'. However, *The Princesss and the Goblin* is usually sold as a children's book today.

In the tale, Princess Irene, at eight years old, discovers her great-great-grandmother, high up in the attic of the castle where she lived. Her great-great-grandmother has been spinning thread woven by rare spiders. The thread is invisible to the eye but can be felt by touch. It is attached to a ring, which the great-great-grandmother presents to Irene. If Irene finds herself in danger, she is to feel her ring to find the thread that will guide her back to her great-great-grandmother and safety. Sure enough, Irene finds herself in great danger one night, on a mountain where fierce goblins live. Remembering her ring, she follows the thread to rescue not only herself, but also Curdie, a miner's son. Neither can see the thread, but the princess can feel it with her forefinger. It guides them away from danger by a very unpromising route that nevertheless leads them to the safety of the great-great-grandmother in the attic.

When they reach the attic, the princess can see her beloved great-great-grandmother, but Curdie cannot. He tells her:

I see a big, bare garret-room – like the one in mother's cottage, only big enough to take the cottage itself in, and leave a good margin all around... I see a tub, and a heap of musty straw, and a withered apple, and a ray of

*sunlight coming through a hole in the middle of the roof
and shining on your head, and making all the place look
a curious dusky brown.*[5]

Irene is distressed by Curdie's response. But surely the invisible
thread is a brilliant metaphor for the invisible connection
between grandmother (or great-great-grandmother) and
grandchild. The story suggests that this connection is
personal, felt deeply by the grandchild or grandchildren,
but not transferable to another person. In whatever form the
'thread' takes, the grandchild can sense its reality, and feel
supported and strengthened by it.

Many grandchildren describe a mysterious connection
with their grandmothers that keeps them safe. A similar sense
of grandmotherly protection is expressed by Mona Polacca,
a member of the American Colorado River Indian tribes of
Arizona and herself one of the 13 grandmothers described on
pages 113-115.

*Grandmother Mona never knew her mother's mother,
who was Havasupai. All she has is a photograph of her
that hangs in the doorway of her home. 'As I go out the
doorway of my home,' Grandmother Mona says, 'I receive
the blessing of my grandmother looking at me. I tell her I
am going to be away from her for a while, look after this
home for me. When I come back into my home, I receive
the welcome of my grandmother looking at me. Though
I've never met her, I have this connection with her.'*[6]

And Ali Cobby Eckermann, an Australian poet, also felt that
her grandmother was a presence that guided her. *Kaanka* (or
kanka) is an aboriginal word for the Australian crow. The
word is based on the sound that the crow makes.

> *Kaanka has become my most defining bird. I believe she is my Nana, still guiding me. When I hear her call, I am immediately inclined to regard my actions and words with kindness, as she instructed. Often she greets me in the early morning as I leave for exercise or work. Most evenings, when the sun is closest to the horizon, she sits outside my house, talking loudly, reminding me of the importance of self-evaluation and responsibility. Kaanka reminds me to remember Nana's teachings, and to stay humble as I journey on my path.[7]*

Another grandmother, Gillian Triggs, who became President of the Human Rights Commission in Australia and then Assistant High Commissioner for International Protection of Refugees at the United Nations in Geneva, looked back at her career and recognised that her own grandmother had inspired her.

> *Sarah-Jane [her grandmother] might have been surprised to know that she has been a driving motivator in my life… I like to think that, in Sarah-Jane's quiet way, she would have supported my outspokenness on human rights… I now understand better the continuing influence she has had on my life, and thank her for it.[8]*

The almost forgotten knowledge of their grandmothers can enable some uprooted and indigenous younger generations to reconnect with their past. The Canadian-born feminist writer Leanne Betasamosake Simpson realised:

> *When I listen to [our grandmothers] talk about pregnancy, childbirth and mothering, I hear revolutionary teachings with the potential to bring about radical changes in our families, communities and nations.[9]*

We grandmothers may not live long enough to learn what aspect of our lives may years later turn into something much needed for our grand- and great-grandchildren. What is our ball of 'invisible thread'? Is it buttons in a worn box, the memory of something we once said, or an anecdote about something we once experienced?

A grandfather's influence may be more obvious. Many work in the public domain. Their 'threads' are usually much more visible. Whereas a grandmother's influence may be hard to identify. That's why the image of an 'invisible' thread seems so appropriate. It may be an influence that we are hardly aware of, even when one of our fingers can feel the thread.

Perhaps grandmothers are becoming more visible. Social attitudes to women have changed. Whether single, married or widowed, women are expected to make their own life choices, as independently as men do. Younger feminists may say that real change has been minimal. But perhaps they cannot imagine how rigid the earlier attitudes used to be. Even younger grandmothers were born into an age in which expectations of women were beginning to be more positive.

We have collectively liberated women from the stigma of being 'the weaker sex', ruled by emotion and not intelligent enough for serious learning. They were expected to depend for their daily lives on the bread-winnings of their fathers and husbands. Although there are plenty who cling to the old misogyny, most people today can see the intelligence, financial capabilities, and strength that women have.

Similarly, we have collectively liberated ourselves, to some extent, from believing that childbirth is always a terrible experience. Some women describe it as excruciatingly painful. But others who have received good preparation beforehand, and kindness and support during the birth, describe the experience as awe-inspiring and empowering.

However, we haven't yet collectively liberated ourselves from the prejudice that motherhood is boring and reduces women's brainpower. Recognition of the sheer intelligence it takes to be a mother still eludes most people.

Surely now it is time to liberate ourselves from the Western stereotype of the ugly old grandmother, with frumpy garments, sagging breasts and false teeth who is constantly forgetting where she left her glasses? This grandmother may exist – but she doesn't have to be reduced to such a demeaning image. She can see herself, and others can see her, differently.

There is a beauty to old age. As a grandmother, many years have been given to her. We can see in a lined face, in worn hands, in unsteady gait, signs of a life well used. And a grandmother still has a future. She hasn't died yet. That huge experience lies ahead of her. And dying, like childbirth, may reveal more wonderful potential than we suppose. It's almost impossible to free ourselves from all the negative prejudices and expectations of death that surround us today. But perhaps as grandmothers we could learn to be more open-minded.

A grandmother has lived. She has contributed. All grandmothers have. Each grandmother has contributed her bit to the significant differences that grandmothers make throughout human history.

And each grandmother can still reach for the invisible ball of thread from either of her own grandmothers, when she needs it. At the same time, she has spun her own mysterious invisible thread which perhaps her grandchildren will be able to sense and use, when they really need it.

References

Chapter 1: The grandmother hypothesis

1. *A Passion for Birth* by Sheila Kitzinger (Pinter & Martin, 2015), page 25.
2. Gaulka-Ma Devi in *Grandmother Power* by Paola Gianturco (Brooklyn, NY: PowerHouse, 2012), page 236.
3. *Mothers and Others* by Sarah Blaffer Hrdy (University of Harvard, 2009), pages 241-43.
4. Hrdy, *op cit*, page 241.
5. Hrdy, *op cit*, page 254.
6. *Women in Prehistory* by Margaret Ehrenberg (British Museum, 1989), page 84.
7. Marjorie M. Schweitzer, 'Introduction' to *American Indian Grandmothers* edited by Marjorie M. Schweitzer (Albuquerque: University of New Mexico Press, 1999), page 15.
8. *Mothers and Others* by Sarah Blaffer Hrdy (University of Harvard, 2009), page 259.
9. *Grandmothers At Work* by Madonna Harrington Meyer (New York University Press, 2014), page 66.
10. *Mothers and Others* by Sarah Blaffer Hrdy (University of Harvard, 2009), pages 260-62.
11. *Grandmothering* by Kathleen Stassen Berger (Lanham Maryland: Rowman & Littlefield, 2019), page xi.

Chapter 2: 'Mum, we've got something to tell you'

1. At the time of writing, an elderly Indian couple had just taken their son and daughter-in-law to court for causing them 'mental harrassment'. The pair had been married for six years without giving them a grandchild. If the case is successful, will it be a precedent for many more?
2. *The Psychology of Grandparenthood* edited by Peter K. Smith (Routledge, 1991), page 9.
3. Ruth Pitt, 'Countdown to becoming a granny' in *Grandmothers of the Revolution* edited by Geoff Dench. (London: Hera Trust, 2000), page 175.
4. Sara Ruddick, 'What do mothers and grandmothers know and want?' in *What Do Mothers Want?* edited by Sheila Feig Brown (Analytic

Press, 2005), page 70.

5. Susan Graff, *Daily Telegraph*, 21 August 2021.

6. Penelope Farmer, 'Introduction' to *Grandmothers* edited by Penelope Farmer (Virago, 2000), page 6.

7. Marjorie M. Schweitzer, 'Introduction' to *American Indian Grandmothers* edited by Marjorie M. Schweitzer (Albuquerque: University of New Mexico Press, 1999), pages 9 and 7.

8. *Grandmothers Counsel the World* edited by Carol Schaefer (Shambhala Publications, 2006), page 42.

9. *Grandmothers talking to Nell Dunn* by Nell Dunn (Chatto & Windus, 1991), page 274.

10. Lorinda Peterson, 'Not a Fairy Grandmother' in *Grandmothers and Grandmothering* edited by Kathy Mantas (Demeter Press, 2021), page 229.

11. *Grandmothers talking to Nell Dunn* by Nell Dunn (Chatto & Windus, 1991), page 225.

12. Letter in *Daily Telegraph*, 6 August 2021.

Chapter 3: One thing we can give as grandmothers is praise'

1. Joan London, 'How Do His Clear Eyes See Me?' in *Grandmothers* edited by Helen Elliott (Melbourne, Australia: Text Publishing, 2020), page 252.

2. Helen Garner, 'Another Chance' in *op cit*, page 10.

3. Arwa Hussein, personal correspondence, 2019.

4. Malika Grasshoff, 'The Meaning of Motherhood Among the Kabyle Berber, Indigenous People of North Africa in *Mothers of the Nations* edited by D. Memee Lovell-Harvard and Kim Anderson (Demeter Press, 2014), page 19.

5. Alice Schlegel, 'The Two Aspects of Hopi Grandmotherhood' in *American Indian Grandmothers* edited by Marjorie M. Schweitzer (Albuquerque: University of New Mexico Press, 1999), page 148.

6. Alexandra Widmer, 'Making Mothers' in *An Anthropology of Mothering* edited by Michelle Walks and Naomi McPherson (Demeter Press, 2011), page 109.

7. June Grassley and Valerie Eschiti, 'Grandmother Breastfeeding Support' in *Journal Compilations*. Wiley Publications, 2008, page 129.

8. Kalia Lyraki, 'Breastfeeding Across Three Generations' in *Breastfeeding Matters*, La Leche League GB, July/August 2020.

9. *Grandmothering* by Kathleen Stassen Berger (Lanham, Maryland:

Rowman & Littlefield, 2019), page 133.

10. *Grandmothers talking to Nell Dunn* by Nell Dunn (Chatto & Windus, 1991), page 110.

11. *Family Jigsaws* by Mahera Ruby (London: Institute of Education Press, 2017), pages 34-35.

12. *Becoming a Grandmother* by Sheila Kitzinger (Simon & Schuster, 1997), page 156.

13. *Grandmothers At Work* by Madonna Harrington Meyer (New York University Press, 2014), page 201.

14. *Becoming a Grandmother* by Sheila Kitzinger (Simon & Schuster, 1997), page 153.

15. Vern L. Bengtson and Merril Silverstein, 'How grandparents influence the religiosity of their grandchildren' in *Grandparenting Practices Around the World* edited by Virpi Timonen (University of Bristol: Polity Press, 2020), page 223.

16. *Grandmothering* by Kathleen Stassen Berger (Lanham, Maryland: Rowman & Littlefield, 2019), page 92.

17. Katherine Hattam, 'Grandmothering and Art' in *Grandmothers* edited by Helen Elliott (Melbourne, Australia: Text Publishing, 2020), page 211.

18. Esther C.L. Goh and Sheng-Li Wang, 'Can Chinese grandparents say no?' in *Grandparenting Practices Around the World* edited by Virpi Timonen (University of Bristol: Polity Press, 2020), pages 239-40.

19. Joan Weibel-Orlando, 'Powwow Princesses and Gospellettes in *American Indian Grandmothers* edited by Marjorie M. Schweitzer (Albuquerque: University of New Mexico Press, 1999), page 193.

20. Lucy Baldwin, 'Grandmothering in the Context of Criminal Justice' in *Grandmothers and Grandmothering* edited by Kathy Mantas (Demeter Press, 2021), page 111.

21. Jaco Hoffman, 'Second-parenthood realities, third-age ideals' in *Grandparenting Practices Around the World* edited by Virpi Timonen (University of Bristol: Polity Press, 2020), page 96.

Chapter 4: 'They grow up quickly'

1. *A Grandmother's Recollections* by Ella Rodman Church (USA, Esprios World Classics, 1851), page 11.

2. *Grandmothers At Work* by Madonna Harrington Meyer (New York University Press, 2014), page 38.

3. Madonna Harrington Meyer, *op cit*, page 234.

4. *Grandmothers talking to Nell Dunn* by Nell Dunn (Chatto & Windus, 1991), page 138.

5. *Grandmothers At Work* by Madonna Harrington Meyer (New York University Press, 2014), page 58.

6. Carol Raye, 'From Ballerina to Grandmother' in *Grandmothers* edited by Helen Elliott (Melbourne, Australia: Text Publishing, 2020), page 218.

7. *Grandmothers At Work* by Madonna Harrington Meyer (New York University Press, 2014), page 42.

8. Jane Caro, 'Pass It On' in *Grandmothers* edited by Helen Elliott (Melbourne, Australia: Text Publishing, 2020), page 42.

9. Letter in the *Daily Telegraph*, 31 August 2021.

10. Jean Stogden, 'The Long March' in *Grandmothers of the Revolution* edited by Geoff Dench. (London: Hera Trust 2000) page 26.

11. *Grandmother's Tales* by Rose Humphries (London: Dean, 1885), Preface.

12. Jaco Hoffman, 'Second-parenthood realities, third-age ideals' in *Grandparenting Practices Around the World* edited by Virpi Timonen (University of Bristol: Polity Press, 2020), page 100.

13. *So this Is Life* by Anne Manne (Melbourne University Press, 2009), page 53.

Chapter 5: 'But [my grandson]'s always busy with his friends or computer'

1. Dovile Vildaite, 'Transnational grandmother-grandchild relationships in the context of migration from Lithuania to Ireland' in *Grandparenting Practices Around the World* edited by Virpi Timonen (University of Bristol: Polity Press, 2020), page 140.

2. Gillian Triggs, 'Grandmothers as Social Activists' in *Grandmothers* edited by Helen Elliott (Melbourne, Australia: Text Publishing, 2020), pages 104-5.

3. Elizabeth Chong, 'At Por Por's Table' in *op cit*, page 87.

4. Esther Sha'anan, 'Beyond the Study Hall' in *Torah of the Mothers* edited by Ora Wiskind Elper and Susan Handelman. (Jerusalem: Urim Publications, 2000), page 494.

5. Joan London, 'How Do His Clear Eyes See Me?' in *Grandmothers* edited by Helen Elliott (Melbourne, Australia: Text Publishing, 2020), page 254.

6. Sara Ruddick, 'What do mothers and grandmothers know and want?' in *What Do Mothers Want?* edited by Sheila Feig Brown (London:

Analytic Press, 2005), pages 79-80.

7. Esther C.L. Goh and Sheng-Li Wang, 'Can Chinese grandparents say no?' in *Grandparenting Practices Around the World* edited by Virpi Timonen (University of Bristol: Polity Press, 2020), page 24.

8. *Grandmothers At Work* by Madonna Harrington Meyer (New York University Press, 2014), page 167.

9. Sara Ruddick, 'What do mothers and grandmothers know and want?' in *What Do Mothers Want?* edited by Sheila Feig Brown (London: Analytic Press, 2005), page 81.

10. *Grandmothers talking to Nell Dunn* by Nell Dunn (Chatto & Windus, 1991), pages 261-62.

11. Nell Dunn, *op cit*, pages 200-201.

12. Justin Hopkins, personal correspondence, 29 April 2021.

13. Jenny Macklin, 'A Thoroughly Modern Grandmother' in *Grandmothers* edited by Helen Elliott (Melbourne, Australia: Text Publishing, 2020), page 155.

Chapter 6: 'As a grandmother, there are two of you'

1. Jan Pahl, 'Our Changing Lives' in *Grandmothers of the Revolution* edited by Geoff Dench. (London: Hera Trust, 2000) page 109.

2. *Grandmothers talking to Nell Dunn* by Nell Dunn (Chatto & Windus, 1991), page 296.

3. Katherine Hattam, 'Grandmothering and Art' in *Grandmothers* edited by Helen Elliott (Melbourne, Australia: Text Publishing, 2020), page 205.

4. *Grandmothers At Work* by Madonna Harrington Meyer (New York University Press, 2014), page 103.

5. *Grandmothers talking to Nell Dunn* by Nell Dunn (Chatto & Windus, 1991), pages 192-93.

6. Celile de Banke, 'Grandmother had no name' in *Grandmothers* by Penelope Farmer (Virago, 2000), page 257.

7. Helen Gardner 'Another Chance' in *Grandmothers* edited by Helen Elliott (Melbourne, Australia: Text Publishing, 2020), page 13.

8. Maggie Beer, 'Food, Music and Soul' *op cit*, pages 110-11.

9. Marjorie M. Schweitzer, 'Introduction' to *American Indian Grandmothers* by Marjorie M. Schweitzer (University of New Mexico Press, 1999), page 6.

10. Marie Dyhrberg, 'Grandparents and Grandchildren, Rights and Responsibility, a New Zealand Perspective'. Paper delivered to *The*

International Bar Association, 2004 Conference, Auckland, New Zealand, page 2.

11. Linda Whelan, 'Where have the Neighbours Gone?' in *Grandmothers of the Revoution*, edited by Geoff Dench. (London: Hera Trust, 2000) page 97.

Chapter 7: The couple relationship

1. *Tell Me A Riddle* by Tillie Olsen (Virago, 1980), page 74.
2. Tillie Osen, *op cit*, page 86.
3. Tillie Osen, *op cit*, page 118.
4. *How Couple Relationships Shape Our World* edited by Andrew Balfour, Mary Morgan, Christopher Vincent (London: Karnac, 2012), page xxix.

Chapter 8: 'She (grandmother) remembered talking to her grandmother'

1. Kate Gavron, 'The Step-grandmother's Experience' in *Grandmothers of the Revolution* edited by Geoff Dench. (London: Hera Trust, 2000) page 68.
2. Auntie Daphne Milward 'A Mima's Story' in *Grandmothers* edited by Helen Elliott (Melbourne, Australia: Text Publishing, 2020), page 55.
3. Jennifer King, 'The Stories of Carolyn King of Parry Island' in *Grandmothers and Grandmothering*, edited by Kathy Mantas (Demeter Press, 2021), page 84.
4. Carol Raye, 'From Ballerina to Grandmother' in *Grandmothers* edited by Helen Elliott (Melbourne, Australia: Text Publishing, 2020), page 220.
5. *The Psychology of Grandparenthood* edited by Peter K. Smith (Routledge, 1991), page 10.
6. Judith Brett, 'My Grandmother's House' in *Grandmothers* edited by Helen Elliott (Melbourne, Australia: Text Publishing, 2020), page 146-47.
7. Harriett Grant, 'Lessons from Yea-Yea' in *Our Grandmothers, Ourselves* edited by Gina Valle. (Ontario, Canada: Fitzhenry & Whiteside, 2005), page 48.
8. Anne Manne, personal correspondence.
9. Elizabeth Chong, 'At Por Por's Table' in *Grandmothers* edited by Helen Elliott (Melbourne, Australia: Text Publishing, 2020), page 81.
10. Jane Caro, 'Pass It On' *op cit*, page 45..

11. Karen Ritts Benally, 'Thinking Good' in *American Indian Grandmothers* edited by Marjorie M. Schweitzer (Albuquerque: University of New Mexico Press, 1999), page 45.
12. Pamela Amoss, 'Coyote looks at Grandmother' in *op cit,* page 95.

Chapter 9: A generation of grandmothers

1. Dr Tedros Adhanom Ghebreyesus, Director-General of the World Health Organisation, in 'Leaders speak out about their concerns regarding older people' on 16 June 2020, www.who.int.
2. *Becoming a Grandmother* by Sheila Kitzinger (Simon & Schuster, 1997), page 8.
3. Sheila Kitzinger, *op cit,* page 41.
4. Helen Elliott, 'Introduction' to *Grandmothers* edited by Helen Elliott (Melbourne, Australia: Text Publishing, 2020), pages 7-8.
5. C. G. Jung, *Collected Works.* Vol. 9, part 1, page 102.
6. *Grandmothers At Work* by Madonna Harrington Meyer (New York University Press, 2014), page 50.
7. Angelita Leticia Orozco De Navas in *Grandmother Power* by Paola Gianturco (Brooklyn, NY: PowerHouse, 2012), page 96.
8. Silvia Nelida Devichi, *op cit,* page 123.
9. Kamla Devi, *op cit,* page 234.
10. Paola Gianturco, *op cit,* foot of contents page and 140.
11. 'Leaders who stay' in *65th Anniversary Magazine* (La Leche League International, 15 October 2021).
12. *The Womanly Art of Breastfeeding* by Diane Wiessinger, Diana West and Teresa Pitman (Pinter & Martin, 8th edition, 2010), page 469.
13. *Grandmothers Counsel the World* by Carol Schaefer (Shambhala Publications, 2006), page 75.
14. Carol Schaefer, *op cit,* page 177.
15. Carol Schaefer, *op cit,* page 26.
16. Auntie Daphne Milward, 'A Mima's Story' in *Grandmothers* edited by Helen Elliott (Melbourne, Australia: Text Publishing, 2020), pages 60-61.
17. Sara Ruddick, 'What do mothers and grandmothers know and want?' in *What Do Mothers Want?* edited by Sheila Feig Brown (Analytic Press, 2005), page 82.
18. *Grandmothers Counsel the World* by Carol Schaefer (Shambhala Publications, 2006), page 90.
19. *Family Networks* by Ross V. Speck and Carolyn Attneave (New York:

Vintage Books, 1974), chapter 2.

20. *Grandmothers talking to Nell Dunn* by Nell Dunn (Chatto & Windus, 1991), page 199.

21. *Grandmothers At Work* by Madonna Harrington Meyer (New York University Press, 2014), page 172.

22. *Grandmothers talking to Nell Dunn* by Nell Dunn (Chatto & Windus, 1991), page 181.

Conclusion: Invisible threads

1. *Why Mothering Matters* by Maddie McMahon (Pinter & Martin, 2018), pages 9-10.

2. *Grandmothers talking to Nell Dunn* by Nell Dunn (Chatto & Windus, 1991), page 267.

3. *Guardian Weekend*, 9 January 2021.

4. *So This Is Life* by Anne Manne (Melbourne University Press, 2009), pages 57, 61.

5. *The Princess and the Goblin* by George MacDonald, 1872. Many editions. Chapter XXII.

6. *Grandmothers Counsel the World* by Carol Schaefer (Shambhala Publications, 2006), page 57.

7. Ali Cobby Eckermann, 'Grandmother's Law Should Never Be Broken' in *Grandmothers* edited by Helen Elliott (Melbourne, Australia: Text Publishing, 2020), page 30.

8. Gillian Triggs 'Grandmothers as Social Activists' in *op cit*, pages 103, 108.

9. Jennifer Brant, 'Aboriginal Mothering' in *Mothers, Mothering and Motherhood Across Cultural Differences* edited by Andrea O'Reilly (Demeter Press, 2014), page 25.

Further Reading

Berger, Kathleen Stassen, *Grandmothering*. Lanham Maryland: Rowman & Littlefield, 2019

Bouvard, Marguerite Guzman ed, *Grandmothers, Granddaughters Remember*. Syracuse, USA: Syracuse University Press, 1998

Church, Ella Rodman, *A Grandmother's Recollections*. USA, Esprios World Classics, 1851

Dench, Geoff ed, *Grandmothers of the Revolution*. London: Hera Trust, 2000

Dunn, Nell, *Grandmothers talking to Nell Dunn*. London: Chatto & Windus, 1991

Elliott, Helen ed, *Grandmothers*. Melbourne, Australia: Text Publishing, 2020

Farmer, Penelope ed, *Grandmothers*. London, Virago, 2000

Gianturco, Paola, *Grandmother Power*. Brooklyn, NY: PowerHouse, 2012

Hrdy, Sarah Blaffer, *Mothers and Others*. Harvard: University of Harvard, 2009

Humphries, Rose, *Grandmother's Tales*. London: Dean, 1885

Kitzinger, Sheila, *Becoming a Grandmother*. New York: Simon & Schuster, 1997

Manne, Anne, *So this Is Life*. Melbourne University Press, 2009

Mantas, Kathy ed, *Grandmothers and Grandmothering*. Bradford, Ontario: Demeter Press, 2021

Meier, Isabelle, *Grandparents: Archetypal and clinical perspectives on grandparent-grandchild relationships*. London: Routledge, 2017

Meyer, Madonna Harrington, *Grandmothers At Work*. New York University Press, 2014

Ruddick, Sara, 'What do mothers and grandmothers know and want?' in Sheila Feig Brown ed. *What Do Mothers Want?* Hillsdale NJ/ London, Analytic Press, 2005

Schaefer, Carol ed. *Grandmothers Counsel the World*. Boston Mass: Shambhala Publications, 2006

Schweitzer, Marjorie M., ed, *American Indian Grandmothers*. Albuquerque: University of New Mexico Press, 1999

Smith, Peter K. ed, *The Psychology of Grandparenthood*. Routledge, 1991

Timonen, Virpi ed, *Grandparenting Practices Around the World*. University of Bristol: Polity Press, 2020

Valle, Gina ed, *Our Grandmothers, Ourselves: Reflections of Canadian Women*. Ontario, Canada: Fitzhenry & Whiteside, 2005

Vickers, Sally, *Grandmothers*. London: Penguin, 2019

My warmest thanks to my brilliant daughter Rachel, to my beloved husband Tony, and to amazing Anne Newman, who all made such excellent edits of the text.

And heartfelt thanks to the five grandmothers who discussed their grandmother experiences with me: Isella Knishkowy, Margaret Brearley, Merrill Carrington, Suzanne Tatz and Vera Kewes Salter.

Thank you, Veronica and Richard Veasey, and Jennifer Marsh, who helped me at the start.

Thank you, Anne Manne and Lauren Porter, for wonderful discussions.

Many thanks to the mothers and grandmothers who have spoken or published on grandmothers. I've only used a fraction of all the interesting material available. Much that I haven't quoted has nevertheless shaped *Why Grandmothers Matter*.

So have memories of my own grandmothers: Hedwig Goldschmidt-Koppel and Regina Jacoby.

Thank you to Rachel and Eric for being such loving parents to Tovi Wen; and to Natasha and Shoël for loving parenting of Anya and Antoshka; and to Darrel for being such a warm uncle to his nephews and niece.

And thank you to Martin Wagner, founder of Pinter & Martin, who invited me to write a book for the Why It Matters series, and suggested *Why Grandmothers Matter*, and Susan Last for her editing and support.

Index

Available from Pinter & Martin
in the Why it Matters series

Series editor: Susan Last

pinterandmartin.com